The Paradise of God

Discover the Biblical Truth About Heaven and
Unlock the Mystery of Life After Death

by
Larry Ollison
B.A., M.A., Ph.D., Th.D.

18 17 16 15 14   10 9 8 7 6 5 4 3 2 1

The Paradise of God
ISBN: 978-160683-867-9
Copyright © 2014 by Dr. Larry Ollison
Osage Beach, MO 65065

Published by Harrison House Publishers
Tulsa, Oklahoma 74153
www.harrisonhouse.com

Dedication

To My Family

My Wife
Loretta Mae Ollison

My Children
Sherrie Renee Kennedy
Raymond Aubrey Ollison

My Six Grandchildren
Raymond Elijah Ollison
Karissa Brooke Kennedy
Larry Joel Austin Ollison
Cassie Shea Kennedy
Aeryn Kaylene Kennedy
Julia Isabella Ollison

Children are a gift from the LORD;
they are a reward from Him.
Psalm 127:3 (NLT)

For as in Adam all die, even so in Christ all shall be made alive. But each one in his own order: Christ the firstfruits, afterward those who are Christ's at His coming.

Then comes the end, when He delivers the kingdom to God the Father, when He puts an end to all rule and all authority and power.

For He must reign till He has put all enemies under His feet. The last enemy that will be destroyed is death.

1 Corinthians 15:22–26

Table of Contents

Endorsements

In every generation there is an evolution of a truth. In Dr. Larry Ollison's new book, *The Paradise of God,* he meticulously reveals all about "Heaven" to a new generation of believers.

Whether you are a seasoned student of the Word of God, or in the discovery stage of the things of the Bible, this book is exciting, revealing, and refreshing for every believer of every age.

Pastor Happy Caldwell
Agape Church
Little Rock, Arkansas

Dr. Larry Ollison is a man well versed in Scripture. Having sat under his teaching, I have found him to be a true teacher of the Word of God. At a time when many Christians seem to be ditching the importance of the Old Testament, Larry brings balance in his teaching so that the Church can enjoy the blessings of the New Testament while appreciating the importance of the Old. His book, *The Paradise of God*, will teach you what you need to know about the future so that your hope can become a sure anchor for your soul.

Pastor Nigel Woodley
Senior Pastor, Flaxmere Christian Fellowship
Gisborne and Hawkes Bay, New Zealand

Someone once told me the definition of a good book is a writer who agrees with you. I want to add to that. It's someone who also improves on what you already know. In his book on Paradise, my friend and fellow pastor, Larry Ollison, takes you to places you have never been in a subject you thought you already knew.

Pastor Bob Yandian
ICFM Trustee

Dr. Larry Ollison's book, *The Paradise of God,* is simply a gift to every born-again believer!!! In his powerful, but user-friendly teaching style, Larry guides the reader on a revelatory expedition into the realm of the spirit...from time to eternity...and on to discover this magnificently exciting and very real "place where God lives."

The Paradise of God is wonderfully illuminating and will catapult your faith to a new level!

Dr. Tom Baggett
Faith Way Ministries
Houston, Missouri

Introduction

Life is short. The dreams and goals of people are many times not accomplished because life ends before they are realized. As a young person, the possibilities and dreams have no limits, but as time passes, many dreams and expectations go unfulfilled. Usually it is not because of a lack of ability, but because of a lack of time.

For the Christian, life on earth is not the end, but the beginning. It is merely the launching pad for limitless dreams and accomplishments, because our future is eternal.

Recently, a famous comedian fell into despair and took his own life. He had great accomplishments in life in the area of theater and comedy, but evidently he felt there was no future and he lost hope. And without hope, our existence is meaningless.

But for the Christian, we have great hope and assurance and a promise from God that is given to us in the Scriptures. Our promise is not vague, but intricately woven throughout the Bible. As a Christian, we are given a detailed account of our future. From the moment we receive Jesus as our Lord and Savior until the unending eons of time in the future, God unveils our destiny and it is good – very, very good.

Your Best Days Are Yet to Come

The Paradise of God is a real place. God's desire for Paradise has always been a place filled with His joy and with the rest and peace that can only come through completion and victory. In these last days, Paradise is filled with the living spirits of the saints waiting for their resurrected bodies.

Upon completion of God's prophetic plan, Heaven will once again be populated, only this time with the glorified, resurrected saints who give Him honor throughout eternity. Rebellion no longer exists in Heaven and it is and will be an eternal place of glory and honor.

There are four instances in Scripture where the Paradise of God is mentioned. The first instance is Eden, the Paradise of God in Heaven, where Lucifer lived before he fell. The second instance of Paradise is Eden, the Garden of God on earth where Adam was placed and told to maintain it. The third instance is under the earth, where the Old Covenant righteous saints went when they died. And the fourth instance of Paradise is in the third Heaven, where Paul visited and the Apostle John had the revelation.

Most people have a skewed vision of what Heaven is or what Heaven was or will be like. They tend to picture angels floating around, some having bows and arrows, and some having harps, but none of them actually having a life. To many people, Heaven sounds like a boring place and there is little desire to go there, although it's much better than the alternative.

Here on earth there seems to be so much excitement. Every day there are new discoveries and adventures. In a nutshell, although life on earth can have its problems, it can also be very enjoyable. When you compare to that the image of eternal life that has been portrayed by the church throughout the centuries through paintings, novels, and movies, Heaven seems to many like a very dull place. When young people compare living on the earth in this age of continually unfolding excitement with living in Heaven, which is often thought of as a solemn place where the atmosphere is somber and the only thing to do is to stand around, it's no wonder that the younger generation is turning away from the future hope that Christianity brings.

The truth is the spiritual kingdom of God, the afterlife or, let's put it this way – the place where God lives – is much more exciting, much more scientific, and much more glorious than anything the earth could ever produce. In the kingdom of Heaven, there will be colors beyond the natural spectrum and inexpressible sounds. Earthly physics will seem like elementary math. The discoveries that can be made in the Paradise of God and the life that can be lived in the kingdom of Heaven will make the earthly lifestyle bland by comparison. It's time that we understand the ecstasy that will come from living in God's kingdom and the pure joy that will be experienced by the continual revelation of the mysteries of God.

In this book, you will learn the biblical truth of what Heaven is really like. You will be taken step by step through the future life of a believer – what they will experience from the time their spirit leaves their body at physical death, to when they receive their new glorified body, through the Millennium, and into the place that

Jesus has prepared for every believer in the New Jerusalem. For the born-again believer, our best days are truly yet to come!

Chapter 1

The Foundation of Understanding

When I was a young boy growing up in Raytown, Missouri, one of my favorite memories was spending the night outside in my yard looking at the night sky.

My yard was large for being inside the city, and covered over an acre. It was the baseball field for the neighborhood boys. Every week I would mow the grass, rake it into a pile, cover it with a blanket, and spend the night sleeping outside looking up at the night sky.

Although I was only in grade school, I knew many of the constellations. The Big Dipper and the Little Dipper were easy to find. But looking at the night sky, the stars seemed to be the same distance from earth. Little did I know that in space, the stars of the Big Dipper and the Little Dipper were not lined up neatly against a black canvas. In reality, they were millions of light years apart and unless you were looking at them from the earth, they were not connected in any way.

As a young boy, space travel was science fiction. Flash Gordon was a comic book character and his travels were all fictional thoughts from the mind. But within a few years of my camping-out experiences, man traveled to the moon and space exploration began.

As it turns out, the solar system consisting of our sun and the planets is not even a speck of dust compared to the known universe. The universe that is observable from earth at the present time is 46 billion light years in radius. That means that light that travels at 186,000 miles per second, or about 671 million miles per hour, would travel for 46 billion years before it would reach from one side to the other of the observable universe. This distance is not the complete distance of the universe, but is only the distance that we have been able to observe. Every time we build a larger and more powerful telescope, we discover billions of galaxies, each containing billions of stars. As incomprehensible as it may seem, there is no end to space.

A few weeks ago, I watched a debate between some of the greatest scientists of our day, and while they did not agree on everything, they all agreed on one reality – that it was impossible for man to grasp a clear understanding of the unfathomable vastness of space and time. While it may be true that our natural minds cannot grasp these things, our spirits can. The Bible tells us that the Spirit of God, the Holy Spirit, reveals the mysteries of God to us. The universe is no mystery to God. After all, He created it; He spoke it into existence. He understands not only the limitlessness of space, but also the nature of time itself. And because He is the creator of the time of man, He knows the end from the beginning (Isaiah 46:10). Through His Spirit and by His Word, we can know our future.

As a pastor, I have officiated and attended hundreds of funerals. I am always saddened when I hear ministers attempting to comfort people using the logic of man. Once I attended the funeral of a man who spent his life as an electrical engineer. At the service, his pastor told the congregation that God took this man because He needed engineering help in Heaven. Another time at the funeral of a young child, the minister said God took the child because He needed another flower in Heaven. And while at one of my relative's funeral, the minister said God always takes the most beautiful. That didn't say much for those of us sitting in the congregation, because the one in the casket didn't look so good!

People of God should never have to make up cute stories to explain what happens to a Christian when they die. The Bible clearly tells us where we came from, and where we are going, and when we will get there, and what we will be doing. While life after death may be a mystery to the world, it should never be for the Christian, because the Word of God clearly reveals to us our future.

In this book, you will discover where we are on the time line of man, how we got here, and where we are going. As Christians, our future is bright and full of joy.

Life is an adventure and the adventure does not stop. It continues without end. In the ages to come, I believe that we will be exploring the universe and beyond. We will not travel at the speed of light, but at the speed of thought, and even though time will still exist, it will be irrelevant because it will be unlimited.

Some people might wonder why God would create a limitless universe. The answer is quite evident. As one of the saints in glory, you will experience limitless traveling abilities to the farthest reaches of the universe with limitless time on your hands. There will be unlimited exploration and unlimited discoveries in the limitless kingdom of God. Life for the born-again believer will be filled with the worship of God and the joys of newness of life that will never grow old.

To understand biblical teaching on end time events, we must first establish some basic principles of interpretation of the Word of God.

Three Foundational Principles

Throughout the centuries, the church has been divided because of doctrine. The word "doctrine" comes from the Greek word *didaskalos* which simply means teaching. Wrong doctrine or teaching has kept the church divided.

Most wrong teaching comes from the lack of knowledge of the Word, and some comes from the confusion that results from listening to the doctrines of demons (1 Timothy 4:1). However, one thing is for sure. Unless you allow the Holy Spirit to give you revelation on three basic fundamental truths, your understanding of the Bible and of end time events (eschatology) will be skewed.

Here are the three foundational principles:

1. Man is a three-part being – spirit, soul and body.

2. Righteousness and holiness are not the same thing.

3. There are three groups of people – Jews, Gentiles, and the Church.

Principle One
Man Is a Three-Part Being

What happens to a Christian when they die? Where do they go? Do they have feelings and an understanding of what is happening on the earth, or are they in a type of soul sleep waiting for the return of Jesus? Are they in Heaven and, if they are, what are they doing? In my lifetime of ministry, these are the most-asked questions when a loved one dies.

To understand what happens when you die and to thoroughly comprehend where you will be during future events, you must first fully grasp and understand the basic concept of spirit, soul, and body.

Spirit, Soul, and Body

Now may the God of peace Himself sanctify you completely; and may your whole spirit, soul, and body be preserved blameless at the coming of our Lord Jesus Christ.

1 Thessalonians 5:23

We are confident, yes, well pleased rather to be absent from the body and to be present with the Lord.

2 Corinthians 5:8

You must know that you are a three-part being. According to 1 Thessalonians 5:23, you are spirit, soul, and body. They are three distinct, different Greek words - spirit (*pneuma*), soul (*psuche*), and body (*soma*). One way of saying it: you are a spirit, you live in a body, and you possess a soul.

You were created in the likeness and image of God. God is a three-part being – Father, the Word (Jesus), and Spirit (1 John 5:7). In the same way that it is impossible to understand the Holy Bible without understanding that God is Father, Word, and Spirit, it's likewise impossible to understand future events without knowing that man is spirit, soul, and body.

Spirit - Your spirit is the real you. When you receive Jesus Christ as your Lord and Savior, it is your spirit that is born again. At that moment, old things pass away and all things become new. When you receive salvation, you become a new creation. The Spirit of God moves inside of your spirit to live, not just to visit, but to live. Your everlasting life begins at that moment. Your spirit will live for all eternity. Your death is recorded on the cross of Jesus (Romans 6:6). Death is now in your past and no longer in your future.

Whoever lives and believes in Me shall never die.

John 11:26

Soul - Your soul is your mind, your will, your intellect, and your emotions. Your soul is where decisions are made on what you think and what you do. Your soul must decide whether to be led by the flesh or to be led by the Spirit. Depending upon what your soul decides, your body will respond.

Body - As a Christian, your body is the temple of the Holy Spirit. Not only is your own spirit contained within your body, but the Holy Spirit also lives within your spirit from the day of your salvation. Your body, while on the earth, is not eternal and it will eventually die and decay. It is like your earth suit. In the same way that an astronaut can only live in space with a space suit, your spirit can only stay on earth with an earth suit. An astronaut can't live in space if his space suit is destroyed, and you cannot remain on earth if your body is destroyed. When your body dies, your spirit must depart (James 2:26).

When we talk about spirit, soul, and body, some may ask, "What about the heart?" Man is a three-part being, not a four-part being. However, the Bible talks many times about the heart of a man. A man's heart is good or evil based upon what he allows into himself through the soul. It is the essence of who you are and is the place where your spirit and soul come together. Jesus said, "Out of the abundance of the heart, a man speaks," (Luke 6:45) and as a Christian, it is your responsibility to renew your mind in order to purify your heart.

When you receive Jesus as your Lord and Savior, it is your spirit that is born again, not your body. Your body will be glorified in the future, but that does not happen until the Rapture of the Church.

Principle Two
Righteousness and Holiness Are Not the Same Thing

Simply put, righteousness is what God does for you and holiness is what you do for God. Righteousness is a result of your accepting His work and holiness is a result of Him accepting your works. Let me explain.

Under the New Covenant, anyone who believes that God raised Jesus from the dead and confesses Him as Lord is saved (Romans

10:9). At the moment that one chooses to believe and confess Him, a supernatural miracle takes place. Old things pass away (sin) and all things are made new. This person becomes a new creation (or creature or new person). Their spirit is born again.

At this point, this born-again person is cleansed from all unrighteousness. If they are cleansed from all unrighteousness, how much unrighteousness do they have? None! They are totally cleansed.

At salvation, the Spirit of God moves inside of the new believer to live forever. Everlasting spiritual life begins. The newly-reborn spirit is possessed by the Spirit of God and sealed by the Holy Spirit himself until the day of redemption (Ephesians 4:30).

God is light and no darkness can enter into Him (1 John 1:5). That's why a Christian cannot be possessed by an unclean spirit. They already have the Spirit of God within them. The reborn Christian's body becomes the home of the Holy Spirit and He does not share His home with demonic spirits.

> *Do you not know that your body is the temple of the Holy Spirit who is in you, whom you have from God, and you are not your own?*
>
> *1 Corinthians 6:19*

> *Whoever has been born of God does not sin, for His seed remains in him; and he cannot sin, because he has been born of God.*
>
> *1 John 3:9*

Because we have the understanding that man is spirit, soul, and body, we can see how the spirit is cleansed and does not sin, while the flesh (body) is still subject to the temptations and addictions of the world.

Paul said that a war was taking place between his spirit and his flesh. While our spirit man is righteous, our flesh must be brought into subjection and become holy.

> *For the flesh desires what is contrary to the Spirit, and the Spirit what is contrary to the flesh. They are in conflict with each other, so that you are not to do whatever you want.*
>
> *Galatians 5:17 (NIV)*

As a Christian matures through the daily meditation on the Word, holiness is increased. However, you are never any more righteous than the day of your salvation. Righteous is what you are. Holy is what you become.

Righteousness is established and is constant. Holiness increases through obedience. We are saved by grace through faith (Ephesians 2:8). We become holy by obedience that activates the grace of God and empowers us to do His will.

Principle Three
There Are Three Groups of People
The Jews, the Gentiles, and the Church

> *Give no offense, either to the Jews or to the Greeks or to the church of God.*
>
> *1 Corinthians 10:32*

Without understanding that there are three groups of people on the earth today, it is impossible to understand the prophetic scriptures in the Bible. While all of the Bible is for our understanding and instruction through revelation, every scripture in the Bible is not written to the Church. Some scriptures apply to the Jews, some to the Church, and some to the Gentiles. Applying a scripture to the Church that is written to the Jews or applying a scripture to the Jews that is written to the Church, brings confusion and misunderstanding of the prophetic word.

From the time Adam was driven out of the garden until the time of Abraham, only Gentiles were on the earth. Then in Genesis 12, God called Abram to build a nation and to be separated from the rest of the world. Abraham and his descendants – his son, Isaac and his grandson, Jacob (Israel) – became the Hebrew nation later referred to as Jews. At the time Jesus was born, there were only these two groups of people on the earth – the Jews and the Gentiles.

However, when Jesus ascended into Heaven on the day of His resurrection and put His blood on the altar, a third group was created. This new group is the Church. Acting as the Son of Man, Jesus became the first man in this new group.

For whom He foreknew, He also predestined to be conformed to the image of His Son, that He might be the firstborn among many brethren.

Romans 8:29

Although Jesus is the Son of God, He completed His work on earth as the Son of Man. There are now three groups on the earth – the Jews (Hebrews), the Gentiles (nations), and the Church (New Covenant saints). You cannot be in two groups at the same time. Every human being is in one of these three groups. You are either a Jew, a Gentile, or part of the Church.

In this current dispensation, everyone is born either a Jew or a Gentile, but when you receive Jesus as your Lord, you are no longer a Jew or a Gentile, but are a part of the Church, the body of Christ (Galatians 3:26-28).

To understand the future of mankind, we must first look at each group and determine what the Bible says about their future.

The Jews (Hebrews)

The spirits of the Jews who were looking forward in faith to the coming Messiah, but died before the resurrection of Jesus, descended into the bosom of Abraham (Paradise). After Jesus resurrected, many were raised from their graves, walked the streets of Jerusalem, and are now in Paradise in Heaven (Matthew 27:52-53). They will be physically resurrected at the Second Coming of Jesus.

> *The graves were opened; and many bodies of the saints who had fallen asleep were raised; and coming out of the graves after His resurrection, they went into the holy city and appeared to many.*
>
> *Matthew 27:52-53*

The Jews who receive Jesus as Lord during the age of grace and before the Rapture are no longer Jews, but at their new birth become a part of the Church. Both the living and the dead will be raptured and receive their glorified, resurrected bodies and ascend into Heaven.

The Jews who believe in Jesus as Messiah after the Rapture of the Church will be hidden in the wilderness of Israel during the time of tribulation on earth. For the last 42 months (3½ years) of the seven years of tribulation, the believing Jews will be safe.

> *But the woman was given two wings of a great eagle, that she might fly into the wilderness to her place, where she is nourished for a time and times and half a time, from the presence of the serpent.*
>
> *Revelation 12:14*

The Jews who are resurrected at the Second Coming and the believing Jews who survive the Great Tribulation will both live on earth in natural bodies in Israel during the Millennium (Ezekiel 43:6-9). Israel will occupy the borders prophesied in the Bible.

The Gentiles (Nations)

Gentiles who converted to Judaism before the resurrection of Jesus became a part of Israel. As long as they believed in the coming Messiah when they died, they would go to the bosom of Abraham and share in the promises of Israel.

Gentiles who receive Jesus as Lord during the age of grace and before the Rapture are no longer Gentiles, but at their new birth become a part of the Church. Both the living and the dead will be raptured and receive their glorified, resurrected bodies and ascend into Heaven.

The Gentiles who believe in Jesus after the Rapture and are either martyred for their faith or survive the Great Tribulation will help re-populate the earth in the Millennium (Kingdom Age). At the Second Coming, there will be a separation between the sheep and the goats. These Gentile believers will be in the sheep category. The Gentiles who do not believe in Jesus as Messiah will be separated as goats, as a shepherd separates sheep (on His right) and goats (on His left) and these unbelieving Gentiles will not live in Heaven or on earth, but will be cast into the everlasting fire, a place of separation until the judgment (Matthew 25:41-46).

The Church (New Covenant Saints)

For you are all sons of God through faith in Christ Jesus. For as many of you as were baptized into Christ have put on Christ. There is neither Jew nor Greek, there is neither slave nor free, there is neither male nor female; for you are all one in Christ Jesus.

Galatians 3:26–28

The Church age began when Jesus put His blood on the altar in Heaven and will end when He appears in the sky to receive the Church at the Rapture. All of the Jews and Gentiles who receive Jesus as Lord during the age of grace (the Church age) are a part of the Church and after the Rapture will live in the Heavenly Jerusalem above the earthly Jerusalem.

The End of the Church Age

When the Church age ends, those who are still living and not caught up in the Rapture will enter into the seven-year Great Tribulation. It will still be possible for them to escape hell. However, they will be under a works judgment and not judged by the grace of God. At the moment of the Rapture, the age of grace is completed and the Church moves to Heaven.

The people who remain on the earth after the Rapture, who receive Jesus as their Messiah during the Great Tribulation and endure until the Second Coming (what we refer to as tribulation saints), will continue into the Millennium, living on the earth (Matthew 25:34-40). At the Second Coming, those who died during the Tribulation as a result of their faith in God will be resurrected. These two groups of people are the tribulation saints and they will live on earth through the Millennium and into eternity.

The Unrighteous Dead

The spirits of the unrighteous dead, who died under the Old Covenant or the New Covenant, and those who will die during the Tribulation and the Millennium, go immediately to Hades and will remain there until the end of the Millennium (Revelation 20:5). They are resurrected after Satan and his army are defeated at the end of the one thousand year reign of Christ. After this resurrection, they will be judged unworthy at the Great White Throne Judgment and cast into the lake of fire, eternally separated from God and His kingdom.

The Promises of God

God promised Israel that there would be a time when He would live with them in Israel (Exdosus 29:45; Revelation 21:3). Likewise, Jesus promised that He would come back for His bride, the Church, and take us to His Father's house. He told His disciples that He was going to prepare a place for them and that He would return and take them there (John 14:1-3). God's word to His chosen people (the Jews) and the promises made to the Church under the New Covenant will be fulfilled.

Throughout the centuries, there has been much confusion concerning end-time prophecy because of the failure to recognize these three distinct people groups. While this failure is often simply a result of a lack of biblical knowledge, sometimes it is because of a stubbornness to think outside of pre-determined denominational boundaries.

However, this is a foundational truth: The Church is not Israel and Israel is not the Church. God has not replaced Israel with the Church. When Israel is mentioned in the New Testament, it is not referring to the Church.

While it is true that New Testament believers are heirs to the promises of Abraham through faith (Galatians 3:29), it does not mean that God withdrew His promises to His chosen people. If He could promise Israel something and then later change His mind, then what security does the Church have that He won't change His mind concerning His promises to the Church? No, God's Word is true and it is established for all eternity. Our eternal existence is only as good as His word.

Life After Death

My dad was a great man of God. He was an ordained deacon in the Southern Baptist church. He served in the 8th Air Force in Europe during World War II and he passed away at the age of 90. At my dad's funeral, there were those who told me they were sorry I lost my dad. Although I knew what they meant, the reality is, my dad was not lost. I knew very well where he was and what he was doing. I know what happened when his spirit left his body.

Through the centuries and even in recent times, there have been many strange doctrines concerning what happens to people when they die. There are many movies that have been promoted by the church that portray incorrect theology. Even some very good family movies with good moral guidelines portray life after death as very bizarre.

Many of these strange teachings have crept into the church. Someone may ask, "How can this be?" Well, the answer is quite simple. Most people spend more time watching movies than they spend reading their Bible. The Bible is the guideline for the absolute truth, and you cannot substitute Hollywood entertainment for God's Word.

So, the next time you read a novel or watch a movie in which someone dies and is trying to earn their wings, or right a wrong that was done to them in this life, or find themselves as a ghost stuck in a certain building or place, know this. While it may be an interesting story, it is not reality because it does not line up with Scripture.

God Wants Us to Know the Mysteries

Some people say that we cannot know what happens after death because God has hidden the knowledge of the afterlife from us. Usually they will go on to say that we must have blind faith and love God and He will take care of us. While that sounds very religious, the truth is God wants us to know the mysteries. There are things that are mysteries, but they shouldn't be a mystery to us because the Revealer of the mysteries (the Holy Spirit) lives inside of us.

In Mark 4:11, Jesus was talking with His disciples. He said to them, *"To you it has been given to know the mystery of the kingdom of God; but to those who are outside, all things come in parables."* A parable is like a story. Jesus was saying, "Look. Those of you who are My disciples and following Me are on the inside. When I tell the story about a man who built his house on the rock and a man who built his house on the sand, to the people on the outside it's just a good story with a moral. But to you who are on the inside, that story will reveal to you the mystery of the kingdom of God."

God wants us to know the mysteries. First Corinthians 2:9 says, *"Eye has not seen, nor ear heard, nor have entered into the heart of man the things which God has prepared for those who love Him."* But we cannot stop there. We must continue reading, because the next verse says, *"But God has revealed them to us through His Spirit"* (v. 10). God wants to reveal His Word to us. That is why He gave us His Spirit..

The Order of Events

Over the years I have noticed that one of the greatest hindrances to rightly discerning end time events is the lack of understanding of the correct chronological order of how these future events for the Church take place. Once this is understood, many scriptures that seemed mysterious or confusing fall into place.

So let's take a moment and review the chronological order of end time events. The following list does not specifically designate the duration or explain the magnitude or impact of these things, but is simply a clear chronological list of occurrence.

1. The Current Church Age

2. The Rapture of the Church to Heaven

3. Judgment Seat of Christ in Heaven

4. Marriage Supper of the Lamb in Heaven

5. The Great Tribulation on Earth

6. The Second Coming of Jesus

7. Satan Is Bound in the Bottomless Pit

8. The Millennial Reign of Christ

9. Satan Released and Defeated

10. The Resurrection of the Unrighteous Dead

11. The Great White Throne Judgment

12. A New Heaven and a New Earth

13. The New Jerusalem Descends out of Heaven from God

14. Eternity

The Adventure Begins

In later chapters, we will explore what the Bible says about Heaven, Paradise, and the afterlife and only count God's Word as the one true truth. Testimonies about life after death that are given by individuals are inspirational, but only what can be confirmed by the Holy Scriptures must be accepted as an ultimate truth.

Study with me as we examine the Holy Scriptures and unlock the mystery of life after death and discover the greatness of the Paradise of God in Heaven.

The Paradise of God

Chapter 2

Creation

In the beginning God created the heavens and the earth.

Genesis 1:1

In the beginning was the Word, and the Word was with God, and the Word was God. He was in the beginning with God. All things were made through Him, and without Him nothing was made that was made.

John 1:1-3

Before time began, before creation, before anything existed, God existed.

A Glorious Place

Heaven is a glorious place and probably the most important place in the universe to God. It is where He placed His throne and is the central location for His command structure in the spirit world (Matthew 6:9).

Look down from Your holy habitation, from heaven, and bless Your people Israel and the land which You have given us, just as You swore to our fathers.

Deuteronomy 26:15

The word "Heaven" is used 692 times in the Bible (NKJV). We know there are multiple heavens. We know this because on one occasion, Paul the apostle visited the third heaven (2 Corinthians 12:2-4) and if there is a third heaven, there obviously must be a first and a second. So, first let's examine the heavens mentioned in the Bible.

The first heaven is the area where we have clouds and the atmosphere containing the oxygen which man breathes. The second heaven is the darkness referred to as space. The third heaven is beyond what we can see. You cannot see God through a telescope, no matter how great is it.

A Different Dimension

When we think about the levels of heaven, so often we think about distance when in reality we should be thinking dimension. Heaven, although it is far away, in the realm of the spirit is actually very close. Think of the distance to Heaven being like window blinds. When they are closed, you cannot see on the other side. Whether something is close or far away, you can see nothing beyond the window blinds. But when you pull the cord and the blinds begin to shift, then everything that is far away and everything that is near can be clearly seen.

Dimensional Shift

When Stephen, who was the first New Testament martyr, was being stoned, he saw Jesus standing at the right hand of the Father in Heaven. I believe a dimensional shift took place and he was able to see to the other side. It's interesting that Stephen alone was able to see, but that's because revelation, whether it be in the Word or in the spirit, is individual.

In the Old Testament (2 Kings 6:8-23), the king of Syria was making war against Israel. The king was troubled because his plans to attack Israel were made known in Israel. And because the king of Israel knew the plans in advance, the Syrian army's strategy failed every time. The Syrian king thought he had a spy in his inner circle. His servant told him that Elisha, the prophet in Israel, was telling their plans to the king of Israel. So he sent his army to capture the prophet of God. When the great army arrived, the multitude of Syrian soldiers filled the hills surrounding the prophet and his servant. The servant of the prophet looked out and saw the army and said, *"Alas, my master! What shall we do?"* (vs. 15).

Then the prophet Elisha said, *"Do not fear, for those who are with us are more than those who are with them"* (vs. 16). The servant looked around and saw two people – himself and Elisha. Then the prophet prayed, and said, *"Lord, I pray, open his eyes that he may see"* (vs 17). The eyes of the servant were opened and he saw the mountain was full of horses and chariots of fire that far outnumbered the Syrian army.

Did the army of God just appear at that moment when Elisha asked for his servant's eyes to be opened? No, the army was already there, it's just that the servant could not see into the realm of the spirit. But when his eyes were opened and there was a shift in the dimension, he could see clearly.

The Bible says that we are surrounded by a cloud of witnesses who are cheering us on and we know that this cloud of witnesses is in Heaven with the Lord. So the reality is this: although Paradise is in the third heaven, it's not really that far away.

Before the Creation of Man

Before the earliest eons of time, the only existence was God. God himself was never created, nor is He an elevated, evolved human, nor is He an alien from space, as some religions teach. God pre-existed everything that was created because everything in the vastness of the universe to the smallest atomic particles was created by His Word, and His Word is a part of Himself (John 1:1-3).

In this eternal existence, God through His Word, created everything. In fact, there is no creation in existence anywhere that was not created by His Word.

In eternity, time does not exist in the way we know it. But in eternity, God created time and a timeline for man. While we live on this earth and experience the passage of the days, to God this linear motion defined by years, centuries, and millennia are only markers for His prophetic Word to be fulfilled.

In the beginning was the Father, the Word, and the Spirit

(the Trinity). He created man in perfection and the existence that mankind knows today began.

The Trinity

Several years ago after speaking at a Full Gospel Business Men's Convention, I was approached by a man who wanted to enlighten me on the error of my teaching. He went on to explain that even though I had mentioned the Trinity in my message, he wanted to inform me that the Trinity did not actually exist because the word *Trinity* is not in the Bible.

While the man was talking to me, I was smiling, nodding my head, and being the polite person I try to be. Then I asked him how he had gotten to the convention center, and he said he had driven there in his new automobile. I told him, "That's impossible! Automobile's don't exist because they aren't mentioned in the Bible." He gave me a puzzled look, we both smiled, and departed. He probably went home and searched for "automobile" in his concordance!

While it is true that the word *Trinity* is not in the Bible, the concept is woven throughout the Bible. The Bible clearly teaches that God functions in three different manifestations and this allows us to understand the completeness of Almighty God.

Through the years, there have been attempts to illustrate how God could be three and still be one. One illustration is that of water (H_2O). Water can be ice, it can be liquid, and it can be vapor. It can freely move between these three forms without changing what it is. While one person may see ice, in another place a person may see steam, while another sees water. And in some cases, all three manifestations can be seen at once. My house overlooks the Lake of the Ozarks and sometimes in the winter, the lake will freeze over. When spring arrives, the ice melts on top and early in the morning you can see steam rising. In other words, you can see ice, water, and steam at the same time.

Another illustration is of a man who is a father, a husband, and a son. Who you are affects how you see the man. To his father, he's a son. To his wife, he is a husband, and to his children, he is a father. But at the end of the day, he is still the same person and all three are one.

While these illustrations show the possibility of three being one and one being three, they still fall short of the magnitude and complexity of God Almighty.

As Christians, we worship one God. We are monotheistic. We worship Jehovah God – the God of Abraham, Isaac, and Jacob – who has always been and shall always be (Revelation 1:8). He is without beginning and without end. He created man on the sixth day and in the days of man on the earth (six days equals six thousand years) God is revealing himself to mankind as the Father, the Son, and the Holy Spirit.

God Reveals Himself

Let's take a look at a few of the scriptures where God reveals himself.

Genesis 1:1 tells us that in the beginning, God created the heavens and the earth. In verse 2, it tells us that the Spirit of God (the Holy Spirit) was hovering over the face of the waters. In John 1:1-3, we are told that the Word (Jesus) was also in the beginning and that everything that was created was created by Him. So here we can clearly see the concept of the Trinity at the very onset of the Bible. And throughout the Bible, God has manifested Himself as the Father or the Son or the Holy Spirit.

In Luke, we are told that the Holy Spirit came upon a young girl named Mary and she conceived and bore a Son. Of course, that Son was Jesus. When Jesus prayed to God, He referred to Him as His Father. Since the Father is the one who impregnated the mother of Jesus (Mary), then obviously the Holy Spirit and the Father are one.

Another time when Jesus was speaking with His disciples, He said, "He who has seen Me has seen the Father. I and My Father are one" (John 14:9; 10:30). So if Jesus and the Father are one, and the Father and the Holy Spirit are one, then the only conclusion is this: The Father, the Son, and the Holy Spirit, these three are one (1 John 5:7).

When Jesus sent out His disciples and gave them the command to evangelize the world, He said that they should teach all nations and baptize the believers in the name of the Father and of the Son and of the Holy Spirit (Matthew 28:19). He was clearly showing the three manifestations of God.

When Jesus was 30 years old, He was baptized in the Jordan River. As He came out of the water, there was a voice that came from Heaven. It was clearly the voice of God and He said, *"This is My beloved Son, in whom I am well pleased"* (Matthew 3:17).

Jesus made another interesting statement in John 8:58 when He stated that, *"Before Abraham was, I AM."* Once again, He clearly stated that even though He was the Son of Man on earth, that He himself was also God Almighty.

There are dozens of other proofs in the Scripture, but they can all be summed up clearly in this one verse. First John 5:7 says, *"There are three that bear witness in heaven: the Father, the Word, and the Holy Spirit; and these three are one."* These three are what we refer to as the Trinity.

Jesus Has Always Existed

Jesus was not created in the womb of Mary. Jesus was, is, and always will be the Son of God. He has always existed. We must understand that at the beginning of time, did not have a human body. He received it 2,000 years ago at the moment of conception. The physical body He had here on earth was created in the womb of Mary. The Scripture says that the Holy Spirit, the spirit of God, came upon Mary and somehow miraculously the seed of the living God was created and placed inside of her and she conceived a child and that child was Jesus.

> But when the fullness of the time had come, God sent forth His Son, born of a woman, born under the law.
>
> *Galatians 4:4*

Jesus, the Son of God, came to earth as a man, but He did not have an earthly father. That's why He could refer to God as His Father because God really was His physical Father. The bloodline follows the male. You can find out who the father of a child is by comparing the blood of the father and the child. In this case, the bloodline of the Father was not earthly, but was pure and without sin. Although Jesus was on earth in an earthly body in the form of a man, He eternally exists in eternity past and future.

Jesus Is Not An Angel

As we have stated previously, Jesus is the Word of God. The Bible clearly tells us that not only is He the Word of God, but that He himself is God. God, through His Word (Jesus), created everything and that includes the angels.

Let's make something extremely clear. Angels were created. God was never created. There was a time that angels did not exist. There was never a time when God (the Father, the Son, and the Holy Spirit) did not exist. To say that Jesus is an angel is to bring God down to the level of His creation and to deny His eternal existence. Any religion, organization, denomination, or cult that restricts Jesus to the office of a prophet is saying that He is a mere man. And any religion that says Jesus is an angel is, by default, saying that Jesus is not God or the Creator. Jesus is the Word and the Word was with God and the Word was God at creation.

The Paradise of God

Seated with Him in Heavenly Places

There is a false teaching that says a Christian will become an angel in Heaven. The Bible does say that a Christian becomes like Jesus. However, Jesus has a glorified, resurrected human body and so will you. In the same way that He was not, is not, and will never be an angel, neither will you. You were created in the likeness and image of God, not in the likeness and image of an angel.

But to which of the angels has He ever said: "Sit at My right hand, till I make Your enemies Your footstool"? Are they not all ministering spirits sent forth to minister for those who will inherit salvation?

Hebrews 1:13–14

He raised us up together, and made us sit together in the heavenly places in Christ Jesus.

Ephesians 2:6

These scriptures tell us that God has never said that an angel could sit at His right hand. God told Jesus to sit at His right hand and that He would make His enemies His footstool. He also says that angels were not invited to be seated with Him because they were ministering spirits that were sent out to minister for those who would inherit salvation. In other words, they were to minister to the body of Christ on earth. But it is interesting to note in this Ephesians Scripture reference that we are seated with Christ in heavenly places. Therefore, once again, it is confirmed. Believers are not angels because angels were not invited to sit at His right hand.

36

The Creation of Light

In the beginning God created the heavens and the earth. The earth was without form, and void; and darkness was on the face of the deep. And the Spirit of God was hovering over the face of the waters. Then God said, "Let there be light"; and there was light.

Genesis 1:1-3

In the beginning God spoke and said, "Let there be light." Genesis 1:3 says, *"Then God said, 'Let there be light,' and there was light."* First John 1:5 says that God is light. Someone may ask, "If God is light, how could He speak and create light?" The answer is, in God's kingdom, everything reproduces after its own kind.

Of course we know that when God said, "Let there be light," that He was calling those things that be not, as though they were (Romans 4:17).

When God stepped into darkness and said, "Let there be light," a more correct translation of the Hebrew would be, "Light be!" When He said, "Light be," there was darkness and in the midst of the darkness, He proclaimed that light existed. What did He see? He saw darkness. What did He say? He spoke light. If God would have spoken what He was seeing instead of what He wanted, there would still be darkness today because He would have had what He said. But, instead of speaking what He saw and instead of speaking what existed, He spoke what He desired and He received His desire. He created us in His likeness and image and expects us to imitate

Him (Ephesians 5:1) and call those things that be not as though they were.

We know when God said, "Light be" on the first day, He was not referring to sunlight, because the sun and moon were not created until the fourth day. "Light be" was God inserting Himself into the darkness. He is the source of all light and life. God is light and in Him is no darkness at all. By inserting Himself into the darkness, God formatted the universe so He could put data into it! He spoke light and life into the universe.

It is also interesting that not only was everything made by the Word of God, but everything was made *for* the Word of God. (Colossians1:16). Some say that everything in the universe was created for man and in a way that is true. However, the Bible tells us that everything was created by and for Jesus (the Word of God). Those who receive Jesus as their Lord and Savior receive equal inheritance. They do not become the Son of God, but they do become joint heirs with the Son of God to receive what He receives.

For by Him all things were created that are in heaven and that are on earth, visible and invisible, whether thrones or dominions or principalities or powers. All things were created through Him and for Him.

Colossians 1:16

The Spirit Himself bears witness with our spirit that we are children of God, and if children, then heirs—heirs of God and joint heirs with Christ, if indeed we suffer with Him, that we may also be glorified together.

Romans 8:16,17

Let's review these truths.

1. God is light (1 John 1:5).

2. God spoke the Word and everything was made through the Word and for the Word (John 1:3; Colossians 1:16).

3. The Word became flesh and Jesus is the Word (John 1:14).

4. In Him (Jesus) was the light of men (John 1:4).

5. Believers are joint heirs with Jesus Christ (Romans 8:17).

God spoke the Word and in His Word was light, life, spirit, and creation. The Word He spoke was Jesus and the words of Jesus were spirit and life (John 6:63). They created and they illuminated.

Man's Days on the Earth

There were six days of creation followed by one day of rest.

Days of Chaos:

>   Day 1 – Light

>   Day 2 – Heaven

Days of the Law:

>   Day 3 – Land, Seas, Vegetation

>   Day 4 – Sun, Moon, Stars

Latter Days:

> Day 5 – Living Creatures of the Sea, Birds
>
> Day 6 – Animals, Man & Woman

Millennium, Sabbath:

> Day 7 – God Rested

The Creation Template

The six days of creation make a clear template of the six thousand years on earth for mankind. Why do you think God created everything in six days and on the seventh day He rested? Why does He say man's days on the earth will be 120 years? Second Peter 3:8 says, *"Beloved, do not forget this one thing, that with the Lord one day is as a thousand years, and a thousand years as one day."* The days of creation are like a cookie cutter template of man's time on the earth. And it has all worked out perfectly so far.

From the time Adam and Eve were driven out of the garden until the time of the Son of Man on the earth, 4,000 years had passed. The first portion of creation (Days of Chaos – days 1 and 2) represents a time of chaos. It was during this time that sin had overtaken the earth and God instructed Noah to build an ark. The earth was destroyed by water.

This was followed by a time (Days of the Law – days 3 and 4) when God set aside a nation and declared that the descendants of Abraham, Isaac, and Jacob were His chosen people. During this time, the children of God lived under the law of God that had been given through Moses. From His chosen people the Holy Spirit came upon a young Jewish girl named Mary and the Son of God was born as the Son of Man on the earth. Jesus brought the availability of salvation to every person, both Gentile and Jew, who would accept and proclaim Him as the Son of God.

The 2,000 year time period from the time Jesus placed His blood on the altar until the time He appears in the sky at the Rapture is considered the last days (Latter Days – days 5 and 6), and that is the time we are living in now.

When Jesus returns and sets up His kingdom for His Millennial reign (Millennium, Sabbath – the 7th day), the fulfillment of man's days on the earth will be complete. Each day of creation represents one thousand years.

Archbishop Ussher, in the 17ᵗʰ century, calculated the date of creation at 4004 B.C. by using the Scriptures. If you research the genealogy of Jesus that is recorded in the Bible, you will find that he was right. From the time of Adam's departure from the garden to the time of Jesus is 4,000 years; the time from Jesus until now is 2,000 years. That is a total of six thousand years. Then adding the one thousand year reign of Jesus gives us a seven day week.

The Scripture tells us both in the Old (Psalm 90:4) and New (2 Peter 3:8) Testaments that with God a day is as a thousand years and one thousand years is as a day. We are expectantly awaiting the return of Jesus so that the coming Day of the Lord (the Millennium) will complete man's timeline so that we can move into eternity with Him.

The Missing Years

The calendar the western world uses is the Gregorian calendar and marks the dates from the approximate birth of Jesus. However, the Jewish calendar is calculated from the time Adam was driven out of the garden. For example, the year 2015 A.D. on the western calendar, corresponds to the Jewish calendar year of 5775. Somebody may say, "That doesn't sound too much like the end of this age if the end of this age is 6,000 years."

I have a book in my library written by F. Jacob Yacovsky, who was born in Ukraine in 1894, that is called *The Missing Two Hundred Years – God's Timetable*. Although I don't agree with all of his assumptions, I think it is interesting that he says the Jewish calendar is off by approximately 200 years. If he is correct, when the western calendar says 2015, the corrected Jewish calendar would read 5975. At any rate, civilization is nearing the end of the sixth day.

To understand God's Word to the Jews, you must be able to understand Jewish thinking. To approach the writings of God with a Gentile mindset will cause you to fall short of many true revelations. With that in mind, let's look at the Jewish concept of the year of Jubilee and see how it compares to the days of man on the earth.

The Year of Jubilee (Leviticus 25)

In Genesis it says that man's days on the earth will be one hundred and twenty years (Genesis 6:3). While it is true that this is referring to the life span of an individual man at 120 natural years, it is also referring to the life span of mankind on the earth as being 120 Jubilee years. Let me explain.

The year of Jubilee is the 50th year. After seven periods of seven years each that equal 49 years (7 x 7 = 49), an additional year is added which is the fiftieth year, or the year of Jubilee (Leviticus 25:8-12). Many rabbis and prophets consider this 50 year cycle as one year. If you count the number of Jubilee years from Adam to now (50 Jubilee years) and multiply it times 120 (the years of man on earth), you get 6,000 years. This represents the six days of creation and the template of man's days on the earth. My, what a coincidence!

According to the Jews, man's days on the earth will be 120 Jubilee years, which equal 6,000 natural years. In six days, God created the heavens and the earth and all that's on the earth including man. On the seventh day He rested. Our Bible tells us that when Jesus returns that He is going to set up His kingdom and in His kingdom, He is going to rule on this earth for one thousand years, or one day. So corresponding to the seventh day that God rested, mankind is subject to the rule and reign of Jesus on the earth. We refer to this day as the Millennium.

A Sign of the End Times

But you, Daniel, shut up the words, and seal the book until the time of the end; many shall run to and fro, and knowledge shall increase.

Daniel 12:4

My grandmother was born in the little town of Climax Springs, Missouri. Until she was a teenager, the only transportation was a horse and buggy. In fact, from the time of Adam until my grandmother was born, man could only travel as fast as the fastest animal he could find. And my grandmother's generation was no exception. But when she was 13, she saw her first automobile. I remember her telling me how amazing it was that it could travel at a high rate of speed up to 20 miles per hour. But within three years of my grandmother's death, man had traveled to the moon and all the world watched it live from their homes. For almost 6,000 years man traveled by animal, but in one generation went from traveling by animal to traveling in rocket ships to outer space.

The Scriptures tell us that in the last days, knowledge will increase. We are truly in the last moments of the last days. Scientists tell us it will take decades to research all of the scientific data that has been collected in the last few years. Knowledge is increasing at a rate faster than man's ability to process it. It's time for the Church to be awake and ready because the sixth day is rapidly coming to an end, and before the seventh day, Jesus is coming for the Church.

Chapter 3

Angels

Before the creation of man, God created the angels. They were magnificent, glorious creatures, filled with beauty and they worshiped God. There are different rankings in the angelic realm. There are archangels, seraphim, cherubim, and other heavenly hosts. In eternity past, all of the angels honored God Almighty with praise, worship, and music, fulfilling one of the duties of their creation.

Eternity Past

In the beginning of creation, Lucifer was in Eden, the Garden of God in Heaven (Ezekiel 28:13). He was covered with beautiful and precious stones of priceless value and within himself, he possessed percussion and wind musical instruments and was anointed from the day he was created. He was the anointed cherub that covers (anoints) and he was established by God himself. He walked freely on the holy mountain of God in the midst of the fiery stones (sparkling gemstones).

God said about Lucifer: *"I established you; you were on the holy mountain of God"* (Ezekiel 28:14). When the Bible talks about a mountain, most of the time the term "mountain" represents "kingdom." So it doesn't mean that Lucifer was on the top of a physical mountain. No, it means he was established in the holy kingdom of God.

In the Hebrew Bible, Paradise is described as a beautiful place of peace and full of prosperity. It is a garden of plenty. In the Greek, paradise simply means a garden. At the time that Lucifer was anointed in Paradise, Paradise was in Heaven. There was unity and peace under the King of the kingdom.

> *You were the seal of perfection, full of wisdom and perfect in beauty. You were in Eden, the garden of God; every precious stone was your covering: The sardius, topaz, and diamond, beryl, onyx, and jasper, sapphire, turquoise, and emerald with gold. The workmanship of your timbrels and pipes was prepared for you on the day you were created.*
>
> *You were the anointed cherub who covers; I established you; you were on the holy mountain of God; you walked back and forth in the midst of fiery stones. You were perfect in your ways from the day you were created.*
>
> *Ezekiel 28:12-15*

Created with a Purpose

God created man for a purpose and He created angels for a purpose. Lucifer got out of his created purpose and that is what caused him to fall. He tried to move himself into the realm designed for man when he attempted to be like God. God was working to get everything ready and in place before He created man when Lucifer decided to branch out on his own.

Angels were never intended to be like God. They were created with a specific function, but that was not to be like God. God is very clear in that He does not want mixing of the seed. We are not talking about mixing races or nationalities or anything within the human race. He wants humans to stay within their domain and angels to stay in their domain. Angels have a purpose and man has a purpose.

The Purpose of Angels

Angels were created to be servants. As stated before, mankind was created in the likeness and image of God. Once again, although man is not God, and will never be God, his creation is within the God family. In fact, numerous times in the Bible, God refers to mankind as His children (1 John 3:1).

Angels, on the other hand, were not created in the God class, but in the servant-to-God class. Their purpose is dual. First of all, for all eternity their purpose is to worship God (Hebrews 1:6). Second, their purpose is to carry out His will, honor Him in every way, which includes assisting and ministering to His children, and to be His messengers to mankind. They carry proclamations to nations, groups, and individuals from God. In fact, the New Testament word *angelos* is many times translated simply as "messenger".

The Purpose of Man

God did make a creation that He wanted to be like Him – mankind. He created us in His image and likeness (Genesis 1:26). Ephesians 5:1 says we are supposed to imitate God. Not only were we made like God, but we are to be imitators of Him. He wants us to walk and talk in God attributes. This is a command. Again, although mankind is not and will never be God, our creation protocol is for us to look like and act like Him.

Mankind also has a dual purpose. First, like the angels, man's purpose is to worship God (John 4:23,24). Secondly, man was created to be in the likeness and the image of God with God's full intention of mankind being sons and inheritors of His blessing (Romans 8:14-17).

"In the image of God" implies that man has some of the same physical attributes in some way the same as God. The Bible refers to the hands of God, His feet, His face, and other features, while the likeness of God implies that man was made to act and respond the way God would act and respond. In other words, we could say that man was created in the image to look like God and in the likeness to have His character.

God expects His creation to live within the boundaries of the purpose of their creation. Although man was created to be like God, the angels were not, and when they demanded an existence outside of their creation and rebelled, God judged them and cast them to earth.

God's Plan Unfolds

God can see the end from the beginning. Before He created man, He created the angelic beings and had put them in position so that when man was created, they would be ministering spirits to God's new creation.

When man was created, it is recorded in Psalm 8 that one of the angels asked, "What is a man, that You've created him a little lower than the angels." Our English translations of this verse say, *"a little lower than the angels,"* but the word there actually isn't angels. The Hebrew word is *Elohiym.* Genesis 1:1 uses the word *Elohiym* and it is translated, *"In the beginning God." Elohiym* is translated *"God"* in the first verse of the Bible! As a matter of fact, out of the 2,606 times the word *Elohiym* is used in the Bible, Psalm 8:5 is the only time the translators translated the word as *"angels"*. So the Bible really says that man was created a little lower than God, not a little lower than the angels.

This fact surprised the angels because they didn't know the position was open! The angel also spoke to God and asked, "Who is this man, and why are you mindful of him?"(Psalm 8:4). In other words, not only was the angel curious as to why God created man, but it further peaked his curiosity as to why God was consistently thinking of man. Of course, it's because God had a plan that He hadn't revealed to the angels as of yet.

One Creator

God's pattern for creation can be seen throughout all living creatures. The angels that are described in the Scriptures have two arms, two legs, heads that turn with two eyes and two ears, similar to mankind. Likewise creatures in the animal kingdom, whether it be mammals, reptiles, or even insects, have characteristics that are very similar.

Recently, several new species of creation were discovered miles deep in the ocean and although these creatures were extremely unique, I thought it was fascinating that they still had two eyes and other similar characteristics found in most other species. Truly, all of creation has one Creator.

In the same way that the Creator expressed Himself through similar physical attributes in His creation, He also expressed Himself in His desire for all creation to willingly worship Him by choice and not through compulsion. While all creation worships Him in ways that we do not comprehend at this time, spirit beings (mankind, angels, and heavenly hosts) must worship Him by choice.

The Free Will of Lucifer

The Bible tells us from the day of his creation, Lucifer was perfect until the day iniquity was found in him (Ezekiel 28:15). When my grandchildren were younger, at some point they each asked me this question: "Why did God create the devil?" Of course, the answer is simple. God did not create the devil. God created

Lucifer and he was perfect in every way. Like mankind, the angels had a choice, and Lucifer became the devil through his own choice.

The Word of God tells us that everything in the universe was created, including Lucifer, but the perfect creation made an imperfect decision to rebel. Although the concept is sometimes difficult to grasp, the truth is that. Although God can look down through the corridors of time and He knows everything that is going to happen before it happens, He still allowed the angels and mankind the ability to choose their own fate.

This is why prophecy in the Scriptures can prophesy a good event or an evil event. It's not that God planned for evil to happen, but He knows the choices men and angels will make before they make them because He sees the end from the beginning (Isaiah 46:10). This is further proven when God said, *"I have set before you life and death..., therefore, choose life"* (Deuteronomy 30:19). He has a plan, but it's our choice as to whether we follow it or not.

The Fall of Lucifer

How you are fallen from heaven, O Lucifer, son of the morning! How you are cut down to the ground, you who weakened the nations! For you have said in your heart: "I will ascend into heaven, I will exalt my throne above the stars of God; I will also sit on the mount of the congregation on the farthest sides of the north; I will ascend above the heights of the clouds, I will be like the Most High."

Isaiah 14:12-14

When Lucifer sinned and rebelled against God, it was because of the pride in his heart. It drove him to proclaim that he would exalt his throne above the stars of God and that he would also sit on the mount of the congregation on the farthest sides of the north.

Because of this, he was cast down and changed from an anointed cherub to a fallen angel and took his place as Satan. In the same way that he, the leader of the rebellion against God, was cast down, one-third of the heavenly host that rebelled with him were also cast down. Satan became the chief demon of all the fallen angels.

Satan and his angels were excluded from the glorious plan of God and confined to one area of the universe until their complete destruction is fulfilled at the end of the Millennium. They were restricted to the area that would eventually be under the authority of man – the earth. God's plan was for mankind to have dominion over the earth and over all of Satan's power.

God could have just as easily cast Satan and his angels to Mars or Jupiter, or even a different galaxy, but instead chose earth. Why? Because without the presence of evil, mankind would not have had a choice and God did not create robots. He created intelligent beings with the capacity to choose and so He placed before mankind life and death, desiring that we would choose life (Deuteronomy 30:19).

As you will see in later chapters, Satan will be bound for one thousand years, and then will be released for a short time back into the earth. Once again, I believe this is to give mankind a choice between good and evil, between God and the devil before the final defeat of the enemy. Once God's plan is chosen, man is then qualified for an eternity with God, free from death and evil (Colossians 1:12; 1 Corinthians 15:24-26).

I find it interesting that when the devil tried to exalt himself and be like God, God cast him down and then made us, mankind, in the image and likeness of Himself. This must have been great humiliation for the devil. Instead of becoming like God, he was rejected and cast down. Then as the whole universe watched, God boldly created mankind in His own image and likeness. That absolutely infuriated the devil. But instead of repenting, he continued in his defiance and his rebellion against all that God loves. To this day, he attempts to destroy God's creation.

When a person receives the righteousness of God in Christ Jesus at the new birth and walks in that righteousness, it's like heaping coals of fire on the head of the devil because when he sees us, we remind him of the One who cast him down.

Pride Goes Before a Fall

As stated earlier, because of pride, Satan decided to exalt himself and place his throne on the sides of the north with the throne of God. He was convincing in his lie that he could be exalted like God. So convincing, that one-third of the heavenly hosts chose to follow him in his rebellion.

Even though Lucifer and his followers believed they could exalt themselves to be like God, their belief did not overpower the truth that God is light and light always overpowers darkness. As a result, Lucifer (Satan) was cast out of Heaven to the earth along with one-third of the heavenly angelic beings who, instead of being exalted and glorified, were transformed into a fallen, demonic existence, confined within the atmosphere of the earth (Luke 10:18; Isaiah 14:12; Ezekiel 28:16).

When Lucifer was on the mountain of God, he was beautiful and full of music. The Scriptures imply that he was a being that led in worship. But there was a day when iniquity (sin) was found in him (Ezekiel 28:15). This iniquity, of course, was the pride in his thinking that he could be like God and rule with God. The error in his thinking was due either to the lack of his understanding, or his refusal to submit to the fact that he (an angel) was not created in the likeness and image of God and was never intended to be an heir, or to be considered a son of God (1 Pet. 1:12).

Pride is a terrible thing and a characteristic of Satan. Pride is something that is never good. There is no such thing as good pride. That's like saying there is good sin and bad sin. No, all sin is bad and all pride is sin. There is not good adultery and bad adultery. There is not good stealing and bad stealing. Stealing is wrong. That's a characteristic of the devil: he comes to steal, kill, and destroy (John 10:10). Pride is not good.

Ezekiel 28 says, *"Your heart was lifted up* [that means it was prideful] *because of your beauty. You corrupted your wisdom for the sake of your splendor..."* (vs. 17 explanation mine). Lucifer was beautiful, but when pride entered in, he wanted to lift himself up instead of using his splendor to exalt God.

When God gives a gift, whether it is singing, acting, teaching, or whatever the talent, it is humility when that gift is used for Him, because it exalts Him. But if the gift is pulled inside and used to exalt oneself, then that is a characteristic of the devil. That's what the devil did. He looked at his own majestic splendor and used it to attract the support of the angels to help him rise up against God, believing he could be like Him.

We were created to inherit salvation, but angels were not (Hebrews 1:14). When Lucifer decided he was going to be like God, he stepped out of his planned design and purpose and took one-third of the angels with him.

The Company of Fools

He who walks with wise men will be wise, but the companion of fools will be destroyed.

Proverbs 13:20

You are of your father the devil, and the desires of your father you want to do. He was a murderer from the beginning, and does not stand in the truth, because there is no truth in him. When he speaks a lie, he speaks from his own resources, for he is a liar and the father of it.

John 8:44

Satan is a con man. A con man convinces his victim that he is telling the truth and that he can somehow put his prey into a higher position without working to attain it. Each year millions of people fall victim to "get rich quick" schemes, perpetrated by con men who, through their deception, are placed in a position of trust where the victim submits his will and resources to the con man. The end result is almost always destruction.

In the same way there are con men on earth, Satan was the chief "con angel." He conned one-third of the heavenly host into believing that by following him, they would be better off than staying with God. So convincing was his con that these angels, who had spent eons of time seeing and experiencing the magnificence of God's Heaven, aligned themselves with the deceiver and put their support behind him. In doing so, they followed in the rebellion led by Satan in which they ultimately lost.

The point I want to make here is this. Satan is the one who came up with the idea, through his pride, that he could be like God and have his throne on the sides of the north. He is the one who deceived his followers and he is the one who led the battle and fought against Michael, the archangel. But even though Satan was the instigator and the leader in the rebellion, every angel that was deceived was likewise cast down to earth and received the same judgment and sentence of future execution that Satan received.

And war broke out in heaven: Michael and his angels fought with the dragon; and the dragon and his angels fought, but they did not prevail, nor was a place found for them in heaven any longer. So the great dragon was cast out, that serpent of

old, called the Devil and Satan, who deceives the whole world;
he was cast to the earth, and his angels were cast out with him.

Revelation 12:7–9

That brings me to this ultimate truth: Those who follow God receive God's inheritance and those who follow Satan share in his judgment.

You Are Responsible for Your Choices

Years ago, I knew a lady whose husband was in prison. She explained to me one day that he was in prison because he had been convicted of murder along with three of his friends. The interesting thing about this story is that her husband stayed in the automobile while his three friends robbed the convenience store. In the process of the robbery, the store clerk was killed. Even though her husband was not inside the store when the murder occurred, by law he still received the same punishment because of his association in the crime.

Faith is a substance in the realm of the spirit that is created by believing God in the physical realm (Hebrews 11:1). Without faith it is impossible to please God (Hebrews 11:6) and through faith, the angels of God are activated (Psalm 103:20). You could say that believing God activates the blessing of God. Likewise, believing the lies of the enemy activates the curse. No one is responsible for what you believe other than you. The angels who were in Heaven, who had experienced the goodness of God, who believed the lie of Satan and based their rebellion upon his lie, still suffered the curse associated with the lie.

Just because you believe something is true, does not make it true. You can believe that gravity does not exist and jump off the top of a tall building with that belief in your heart. But regardless of how strong your belief is, if the belief is rooted in deception and lies, it will bring destruction. And that's what happened to the angels who followed Lucifer in his rebellion.

Angels of God and Fallen Angels

At the time the heavenly hosts were cast out of Heaven, they were divided into two groups – the angels of God and the fallen angels. The angels of God contained two-thirds of the heavenly hosts who remained obedient and with God. The fallen angels, one-third of the original heavenly hosts, followed Lucifer in his rebellion and were cast down to the earth with him. They were judged with him and all became fallen angels or demonic, unclean spirits.

Although the Bible says that there are so many angels that they cannot be numbered (Hebrews 12:22), and although it may seem devastating that one-third of the heavenly host rebelled in Heaven and were cast out by Michael (the archangel) and his angels, we must realize that two-thirds of the angelic host chose not to rebel, but to complete the mission of their creation which was to worship God (Revelation 7:11) and assist mankind (Hebrews 1:14). There is no shortage of good angels.

It's important to note here that God did not remain God because He received a majority of the votes of loyalty from the angels. The kingdom of God is not a democracy. It is a kingdom and in a kingdom, the king rules. Whether you agree with the king or disagree with the king is irrelevant. His word is law. His word is final. His word rules. We must understand that even if 100% of the angels had followed Lucifer, they would have still been cast out of Heaven. God created the angels, He is all powerful, and the created is not greater than the Creator (John 13:16).

God is the life and light of the universe and without Him, the universe cannot exist.

The Spiritual Forces of Faith and Fear

Faith and fear are opposites. In the same way that hot and cold, up and down, east and west, are opposites, likewise faith and fear are opposites. They cannot both be active at the same time. In my airplane, there is a gauge that gives me the rate of ascent or the rate of descent. It tells me how quickly I am ascending or it tells me how quickly I am descending. There is only one gauge for this function because I cannot be doing both at the same time. If I am going up, I am not going down. And if I am going down, I am not going up. Up and down are opposites and you cannot be doing both at the same time.

Faith and fear are the two forces in the spirit realm that activate angelic assistance. Faith activates the angels of God and fear activates fallen angels (demonic spirits). Romans 10:17 says that faith comes by hearing when you hear the Word of God. Of course we know that to activate faith, you must believe what God says.

Likewise, fear comes from hearing, but it comes by hearing the words of the enemy and when you believe what he says, it activates the fear.

Activating Spiritual Forces

Psalm 103:20 says that angels (the angels of God) are mighty in strength and that they are standing by waiting to hear the voice of God's Word and when they hear it, they act upon it. As a Christian, you are the voice of God's Word on the earth today. When you say what He says, it activates His angels to minister to you in the area of the promise in His Word that you have spoken and believed. In other words, when you say and confess what God says about you, it activates the angels of God to bring it to pass.

When something looks impossible in your life, as a Christian, you cannot base your life upon the way things look. Instead, you must walk by faith and not by sight. In doing this, you will say what God says about your circumstances instead of saying the way things look.

For example, when it looks like a situation or circumstance in life is overpowering and that your defeat is imminent, remember that greater is He that is in you than he that is in the world (1 John 4:4). Remember that your faith in God's Word will bring a victory (1 John 5:4). When the angels of God hear you speak the Word of God, they stand up and operate in the purpose of their creation, which is to minister to those who will inherit salvation (Hebrews 1:14). The power of one angel can overpower all of the world.

However, on the other hand, if you speak the negative words of fear, these words fuel the demonic realm and by relinquishing your authority that comes through the words of faith, you, by default, allow the enemy to bring destruction. If God's Word says you can do all things through Christ who strengthens you (Philippians 4:13), but the words coming out of your mouth are, "I can't do this. We are going to be destroyed. There's no hope for us," you nullify the authority you've been given over the power of the enemy and open the door for the enemy to enter your house.

Speak to the Mountain

Jesus said that if we would speak to the mountain, that it would move. However, He followed with a qualifying statement. Immediately after stating that the mountain would be removed after we commanded it to be cast into the sea, Jesus said this. He said if we believe in our heart that the words we say would come to pass, then we would have whatever we said (Mark 11:23).

What does this mean? This means that even though you may say the right words, if you don't believe them in your heart, they are empty and they are of no effect. So how do we speak God's promises for us with authority and belief knowing that what He said is true? Well the answer is quite simple and clear. There is only one verse in the Bible that tells us how faith comes. And that is in Romans 10:17 and it says, *"So then faith comes by hearing, and hearing by the word of God."*

We know for a fact that if you hear something enough times, you believe it. This is where we get the term "brainwashed." Christians need to get their brains washed with the Word of God (Romans 12:2). Instead of filling themselves with the lies of the enemy, their minds must be renewed with the Word of God. Through this daily washing of the Word in the realm of their souls, the belief in God's Word that's in our hearts will activate the words that we speak, which in turn will activate the angels of God to cause that Word to come to pass.

Angelic Assistance is Available

"Are they not all ministering spirits sent forth to minister for those who will inherit salvation?" (Hebrews 1:14). Angels are here to help us, not to scare us. They can help us in the same way they helped the Christians in the Bible.

In Acts 12, Herod the king arrested Peter and put him in prison and assigned four squads of soldiers to guard him. Peter was in an impossible situation. But the church was praying, and in the middle of the night an angel came to him and got him out of prison.

As a Christian, you have the power of Heaven in the form of angelic assistance available to you that can deliver you from any attack of the enemy (Psalm 34:19). Whatever the problem, whatever the circumstance, regardless of how great it is or how desperate things may look, the angels of God are standing by waiting to hear the voice of His Word so that they can leap to your aid to deliver you.

Angels

For He shall give His angels charge over you, to keep you in all your ways. In their hands they shall bear you up, lest you dash your foot against a stone.

Psalm 91:11,12

You must understand this. As a Christian, you have been given authority over all the power of the enemy and that power is activated when you speak the Word of God in faith. In one night one angel sent from God destroyed 185,000 enemy soldiers coming against the nation of Israel. You have multitudes of angels waiting to deliver you today (Isaiah 37:36). Know your authority, speak the Word of God and be delivered.

The Call of Abraham

In the passage of time in the year 1948 on God's timetable, a man was born named Abram. Abram lived in the city of Ur and was called out by God to move into a new land. God told him that He would make him a great nation, that he would be blessed and that his name would be great and through him all the nations of the earth would be blessed. God told him that He would bless those that bless Abram and that He would curse those who cursed him.

Now the LORD had said to Abram: "Get out of your country, from your family and from your father's house, to a land that I will show you. I will make you a great nation; I will bless you and make your name great; and you shall be a blessing. I will

63

bless those who bless you, and I will curse him who curses you;
and in you all the families of the earth shall be blessed."

Genesis 12:1-3

So Abram followed the instructions of the Lord. He was 75 years old and he departed from Haran. He took with him, Sarai, his wife and his nephew, Lot. They took all the possessions they had and gathered the people that they were in charge of and they departed to go to the land of Canaan.

After passing through Egypt, Abram, Sarai, and Lot moved toward the south. Abram was extremely rich. He had livestock, silver, and gold. As he journeyed to the south as far as Bethel, he settled between Bethel and Ai. Lot who was traveling with him, also had flocks and herds and many servants and it appeared that the land was not able to support both of them in the same area. To add to the problem, there was strife between the herdsmen of Abram and Lot.

So Abram told Lot that in order for there to be no strife between them and their herdsmen, "Why don't you choose where you would like to live and I'll take the rest. If you take the land on the right, I'll take the land on the left. If you take the land on the left, I'll take the land on the right."

So Lot looked at the plain of Jordan as he saw that it was well watered like the garden of the Lord. So he chose for himself all of the plain of Jordan. Lot journeyed east and separated himself from Abram. And while Abram dwelt in the land of Canaan, Lot dwelt in the cities of the plain and he pitched his tent even as far as Sodom.

Sodom and Gomorrah

The men of Sodom were wicked and sinful. In the passage of time, it came about that the cities of Sodom and Gomorrah were going to be destroyed because of their blatant sin. Lot and his family, who had moved into the city of Sodom, were visited by two angels. As the angels entered the gate of the city of Sodom, Lot was sitting near the gate. When he discovered that the two angels were going to spend the night in the open square, he strongly insisted that they should stay at his house. He knew that the men of the city had fallen into such depravity that the angels of God would be assaulted.

They called to Lot, "Where are the men who came to you tonight? Bring them out to us so that we can have sex with them."

Genesis 19:5 (NIV)

After preparing a feast for the angels, and before Lot's household retired for the night, the men of the city of Sodom both old and young from every portion of the city surrounded Lot's house and they demanded that Lot send the angels outside so that they could have sexual relations with them. Lot stepped through the door to the outside and shut the door behind him. He was so fearful of what would happen to the angels that he offered the men his daughters. But they refused and pressed hard against Lot, attempting to break down the door.

The angels reached out their hand and pulled Lot back inside the house with them and shut the door. Then the angels struck the men who were at the door with blindness. Even in their blindness, they still attempted to find the door and enter in, but could not.

Later, Lot and his family left the city and the cities of Sodom and Gomorrah were destroyed as fire and brimstone rained out of the sky. The cities burned and smoke went up into the sky like the smoke of a furnace. Lot and his family, except for his wife, escaped.

Here is the point I'd like to make. Although the people of Sodom and Gomorrah were moved by evil to destroy God's creation through homosexuality, the angels of God prevailed over the wickedness of the land. Although it may appear that the fallen angels can deceive and manipulate man, they are no match for the angels of God.

Features and Abilities of Angels

Then he made them a feast, and baked unleavened bread, and they ate.

Genesis 19:3

And they struck the men who were at the doorway of the house with blindness, both small and great, so that they became weary trying to find the door.

Genesis 19:11

In this passage in Genesis 19, we discover some very interesting facts about the features and abilities of angels. First, the two angels of God that entered into Sodom looked like natural men to the people of Sodom. In fact, they looked so perfect that the homosexual men of Sodom desired them sexually. But while the reality that they were angels was hidden from the men of Sodom, it was revealed to Lot.

We see that all through history there is greater revelation to the righteous.

It's also interesting to note that the angels ate food and desired rest for the night. When evil pushed toward them, by stretching forth their hand they had the power to blind the men of the city. They were in the form of men, without wings, and wore the normal clothing of the day.

Although this event took place in Old Testament times, likewise the Church was told by Paul that Christians should treat strangers kindly because of the possibility that the stranger might be an angel. This would indicate that the likeness of an angel to man is so close that to the natural eye, they are indistinguishable (Hebrews 13:2).

God has always planned for man and woman to reproduce and create life. When a man has sexual relations with a man, or when a woman has sexual relations with a woman, life is not created. If everyone in that generation follows that plan, then that generation becomes the last generation to exist. This is why God commanded in Leviticus 18:22 that a man should not have sex with another man as he would with a woman. In fact, in that scripture God calls it an abomination.

You shall not lie with a male as with a woman. It is an abomination.

Leviticus 18:22

Anything that goes contrary to the plan of God is not of God and is sin. Anytime you exalt a plan above the plan of God, you are saying that you do not believe God and according to Romans 14:23, not believing God is a sin.

> *But he who doubts is condemned if he eats, because he does not eat from faith; for whatever is not from faith is sin.*
>
> *Romans 14:23*

God Has Not Changed

> *God is not a man, that He should lie, nor a son of man, that He should repent. Has He said, and will He not do? Or has He spoken, and will He not make it good?*
>
> *Numbers 23:19*

Although today the Church is living in the age of grace, we cannot use grace as an excuse to sin (Romans 6:15). Even though God is a good God and the Father of all good gifts (James 1:17) and although He loves us so much that He sent His Son, Jesus, to die in our place, what He likes and what He dislikes throughout the ages of time has not changed.

Currently in the United States of America, there is a trend to accept many things legally that the Bible says God considers an abomination. But regardless of the laws of man, God's personality and desire has not changed. The things He did not like during the time of Sodom and Gomorrah, He clearly did not like them 2,000 years ago at the writing of the New Testament, which was inspired by His Holy Spirit. And we know that since God has not changed (Hebrews 13:8) that the things He did not approve of in the past, He does not approve of them today.

As Christians, we must make a choice. Just because something is legal in the natural government, does not mean that it is acceptable in the kingdom of God. God does not change His plan for mankind to line up with rules and regulations dictated by man.

Let's take a look at some basics concerning the spirit realm and the things of demons.

Five General Facts About Fallen Angels

1)   Satan is a fallen angel (Luke 10:18).

Satan attempted to be like God, but he never accomplished his goal. Although he is a ruler over the fallen angels and a god of this world until he is bound (John 12:31), he will never be like Jehovah God. He was created by God, he was created as an angel and he was cast out.

2)   Satan was created by God and is not equal to God in any way (Ezekiel 28:13).

God created Lucifer. Lucifer sinned and was cast to the earth. Jesus defeated the works of Satan 2,000 years ago and Satan's future destiny is sealed. Satan is an angel and not equal to God.

3)   God is all-powerful and has already won the war with the devil (Colossians 2:15).

If God has already won the war, then why do we have to deal

with the devil? Basically, this is what has happened. God, through His Son, Jesus, has defeated the devil and shown us by example that we can do the same things He did. The devil has been judged and is waiting for the execution of his sentence. You might say the devil is on death row. The day is coming when God's angel will chain him in the bottomless pit. But until that happens, we still have to deal with him.

4) Christians have been given authority over the kingdom of darkness and should not fear it (Luke 10:19).

The devil's kingdom is the kingdom of darkness. You have nothing to fear when it comes to demonic spirits. Over the years, there have been demonic attacks on me while I've been preaching. There have been people who have come up out of the congregation and physically attacked me with the intention of taking me down. It's not uncommon to see demonic manifestations. But we simply stand up and command them to stop, and they have to obey. When you stand nose to nose with a demonic spirit, it must back down because you are the one with the authority.

5) Fallen angels are restricted (Revelation 12:9).

The fallen angels that were cast to the earth with Satan were not given the liberty of travel beyond the place of their restriction. They are confined to the earth and will remain there until the Millennium. After the one thousand year reign of Christ, they will be cast into the everlasting fire, along with their leader, Satan.

Five General Facts About the Angels of God

1) God's angels are created beings that answer to God's Word (Psalm 103:20).

2) The angels of God freely move about in Heaven and on earth, assisting God and those who will inherit salvation (born-again believers) (John 1:51).

Then he dreamed, and behold, a ladder was set up on the earth, and its top reached to heaven; and there the angels of God were ascending and descending on it.

Genesis 28:12

3) The angels of God rejoice when a sinner repents (Luke 15:10).

The angels of God obviously honor the same goals and desire of the Father. When righteousness prevails, they rejoice.

4) Angels are not to be worshiped.

All through the Scriptures, we are taught that angels were created as ministering spirits and servants to those who will inherit salvation. They are activated by the Word of God to implement God's will. Christians are joint heirs with Christ and are to rule and reign with Him throughout eternity. The saints will judge angels and are specifically told that the worship of angels would defraud the believer of their prize.

Let no one cheat you of your reward, taking delight in false humility and worship of angels.

Colossians 2:18

5) Angels can take on human form.

Angels do not become human. They cannot change their existence from angel to man. However, they can have the appearance of a human and remain undetected as an angel.

Do not forget to show hospitality to strangers, for by so doing some people have shown hospitality to angels without knowing it.

Hebrews 13:2 (NIV)

They were looking intently up into the sky as he was going, when suddenly two men dressed in white stood beside them.

Acts 1:10

Chapter 4

Authority Over the Kingdom of Darkness

He who sins is of the devil, for the devil has sinned from the beginning. For this purpose the Son of God was manifested, that He might destroy the works of the devil.

1 John 3:8

Before we go any further in our discussion about the kingdom of darkness, which includes fallen angels, or demonic spirits, we must anchor this truth. The kingdom of darkness is subject to Jesus, the name of Jesus, and if you are a born-again believer, it is subject to you. The power of God will never yield to the kingdom of darkness and as a born-again believer, the Holy Spirit of God lives in you and you have been given authority by Jesus himself over all the power of the enemy. You have nothing to fear. The kingdom of light always overpowers the kingdom of darkness.

The world, through novels, theater, and movies, portrays the kingdom of darkness as all powerful. The entertainment media often portrays the people of God as being overpowered by demonic spirits, confused, and wondering why the holy water and the Bible can't stop the demonic attack. A Christian should have a clear understanding of the difference between theatrical entertainment and the truth contained in the Word of God. The truth is contained in Jesus' statement where He said, "I give you all authority over the power of the enemy and nothing shall by any means hurt you" (Luke 10:19).

Does the enemy have power? Yes, of course he does, because Jesus said so. But the good news is as a believer, you have been given authority over anything the enemy has in his arsenal of weapons. Your words of faith can cast out any demonic spirit and your shield of faith will protect you from any attack that comes against you.

The Attempt to Destroy God's Plan

And He said to them, "I saw Satan fall like lightning from heaven."

Luke 10:18

How you are fallen from heaven, O Lucifer, son of the morning! How you are cut down to the ground, you who weakened the nations!

Isaiah 14:12

When Satan was cast to the earth and his angels with him, we see that he immediately tried to destroy God's prophetic plan for man by tempting and bringing to pass the sin of Adam in the Garden of Eden. Although Satan may have thought he had stopped God's plan from coming to pass, he underestimated the grace and mercy of the Lord God. God did not give up on His creation. His plan for the redemption of man had been established before the foundation of the earth.

Sin of the Fallen Angels

In the years that followed Adam's removal from the garden, murder entered into the hearts of men and great evil came upon the face of the earth. From the institution of sun worship through Nimrod and the depravity of man, the fallen angels attempted to pollute the bloodline of man. God caused a great flood to come upon the earth that destroyed all living flesh except for Noah, his wife, his three sons and their wives.

> *When human beings began to increase in number on the earth and daughters were born to them, the sons of God saw that the daughters of humans were beautiful, and they married any of them they chose. Then the LORD said, "My Spirit will not contend with humans forever, for they are mortal; their days will be a hundred and twenty years."*
>
> *Genesis 6:1–3 (NIV)*

Since the angels who were involved in this sinful act were spirit beings rather than flesh and since flood waters will not destroy the spirit, they received a different punishment. The fallen angels who were involved in this sin were cast down to hell and placed in chains of darkness where they will remain until their ultimate judgment at the end of the Millennium.

...God did not spare the angels who sinned, but cast them down to hell and delivered them into chains of darkness, to be reserved for judgment; and did not spare the ancient world, but saved Noah, one of eight people, a preacher of righteousness, bringing in the flood on the world of the ungodly.

2 Peter 2:4,5

The Power of God Is Greater

You believe that there is one God. You do well. Even the demons believe—and tremble!

James 2:19

When Jesus sailed to the land of the Gadarenes, as He stepped out of the boat onto the land, there was a man who had been demon possessed for a long time waiting for Him. He was naked and lived in the tombs nearby. This man was so violent that he was kept under constant guard and was literally shackled and chained so that he would not break free. The superhuman strength he was given by the demons allowed him to break free from the chains and the demons drove him into the wilderness.

When Jesus commanded the unclean spirit to come out of the man, the demon said, *"What have I to do with You, Jesus, Son of the Most High God? I beg you, do not torment me"* (Luke 8:28). Then Jesus asked the demon, *"What is your name?"* (Luke 8:30). His response was that his name was Legion because he was possessed by many demons. The Roman legion varied greatly over time, but typically was composed of as many as 6,000 soldiers.

The demons begged Jesus that He would not command them to go out into the abyss. There was a herd of swine feeding close by on a mountain and the demons begged Him to allow them to enter the swine. Jesus gave them permission. The Bible says that when the demons went out of the man and entered the swine, the swine ran violently into the lake and they were drowned.

It's interesting that Jesus said in Matthew 12:43-45 that when an unclean spirit goes out of a person that it passes through dry places trying to find rest but can't find any. The herd of pigs may have appeared to be a dry place to the demons, but much to their surprise they ended up in the water. It has been humorously said by some, "Be careful what you ask for." The demons, seeking a dry place, ended up in the abyss after all.

When all of this occurred, it was not a private event. There were people who saw what happened and they went into the nearby city and told this story. And a crowd came out to see what had happened. They came to Jesus and found the man that had been terrorizing their city sitting at the feet of Jesus. He was fully clothed and in his right mind. You would have thought they would have been very thankful for what Jesus had done, but instead they became fearful and people from the entire region asked Him to leave. The Bible says they were seized with great fear.

So Jesus got into the boat and He left. The man who had been demon possessed actually wanted to leave with Jesus, but Jesus instructed him to return home and to tell about the great things that God had done for him. And that's exactly what he did.

We see a great truth in this passage. Regardless of the number of demons coming against a single believer, the power of God is greater than a legion of demons.

Can a Christian be Demon-Possessed?

Through several decades of ministry, both traveling and as pastor, many have asked if a Christian can be possessed by a demonic spirit. The answer to the question is no, and here is why.

Under the Old Covenant, man did not have the Holy Spirit living inside of him. The Holy Spirit came upon prophets, priests, and kings, and there were times when men and women of God would be filled with the Holy Spirit. But these times were for a specific purpose and the moving of the Holy Spirit in their lives was an event, or we might say, a visitation. But it wasn't until after the sacrifice of Jesus on the altar in Heaven that a way was made for man to be indwelt with the Spirit of God himself.

Once Jesus made the way possible, anyone who believed that He was the Son of God and that God raised Him from the dead and confessed it became born again and a part of the Church (the body of Christ) (Romans 10:9). At the moment of salvation, the Holy Spirit moved inside the spirit of the new believer and took up residence. It was not a visitation, it was a habitation. From that point throughout eternity, the Spirit of God resides there.

The Bible tells us that God is light and in Him is no darkness. The Bible also says that at salvation our spirit is made righteous, cleansed from all unrighteousness. Paul said in 1 Corinthians 6:19

that our bodies are the temple of the Holy Spirit. God will not allow a demonic spirit in His temple. While it is true that our flesh still sins, our spirit does not. That's what the scripture means that says, *"Whoever has been born of God does not sin, for His seed remains in him; and he cannot sin, because he has been born of God"* (1 John 3:9). But your soul and your flesh have not been born again and are still subject to the torments of unclean spirits.

The Apostle Paul put it this way. He said that his spirit and his flesh were at war with each other (Galatians 5:17). Why would he say that? Simply because his spirit had been born again and the Spirit of God lived in him. The Spirit of God is light and the Spirit had sealed him until the day of redemption. However, his flesh had not yet been redeemed and was subject to the temptations of the world.

Keep in mind, the original question was, "Can a Christian be demon possessed?". The answer is no, but a person who is not born again can be. Why? Because they do not have the Spirit of God living inside of them. So simply put, non-Christians can be demon possessed but Christians cannot, although through the works of the flesh, a Christian can allow themselves to be oppressed and tormented from the outside influence of unclean spirits.

No Fear

Behold, I give you the authority to trample on serpents and scorpions, and over all the power of the enemy, and nothing shall by any means hurt you.

Luke 10:19

Although demonic spirits are still on the earth, the Christian should not fear them. As you travel throughout life and encounter demonic spirits either in someone else or one who is trying to torment you, exercise your authority over them without fear and do not allow them to waste your time.

Jesus and the apostles dealt severely with demonic spirits as they encountered them, but did not set up a ministry that specialized in exorcism. One of the main ways that a demonic spirit can cause a Christian to not fulfill the work that God has given them to do is by distracting them and refocusing their time and actions on the kingdom of darkness. Over the years, I have seen men and women of God waste their time trying to change someone who was pretending to want deliverance. This distraction became an obsession that kept them from fulfilling the complete call of God for their lives.

When Jesus got off the boat, He didn't say "Where are the demons?" They found Him. Trust me, if you are walking in the anointing of God, the demons know who you are.

The seven sons of the Jewish priest, Sceva, tried to cast out demons, but they did not have the authority. The demons responded to their attempt to cast them out: "We know who Paul is and we know who Jesus is, but we don't know who you are." The result was the demons leaped upon the sons of the Jewish priests, ripped off their clothes, and beat them (Acts 19:13-16).

Once again, as a Christian, this will not happen to you because you have been given authority over the demons and they are subject to you (Luke 10:17).

Mark 16:9 says, *"Now when He rose early on the first day of the week, He appeared first to Mary Magdalene..."* When Jesus first resurrected, the first person He appeared to was Mary Magdalene, *"...out of whom He had cast seven demons."* This was referring to the past, before His resurrection. What does that tell us? That He cast seven demons out of Mary Magdalene. So Mary Magdalene, although she was a great follower of Jesus, evidently had a horrible past, because she had seven demonic spirits inside her. That lets us know that deliverance is possible. You can get delivered out of a horrible lifestyle and you can become a great man or woman of God.

Take Your Authority

When someone is given authority in a certain area, they can either use it or not use it. In a classroom, the teacher is given authority by the school board over the students in their class. Whether they use it or not is their own decision. I've seen classes where the students have run rampant and created chaos in the classroom. It wasn't that the school board had not given the teacher authority, the teacher just didn't know how to use the authority.

As Christians, we must know how to use the authority that's

been given to us by God so that we don't allow the devil to run rampant over us.

Now in no way is it my intention to glorify the devil or the works of the devil. But Paul told us that we shouldn't be ignorant of the devil's devises so that he can't take advantage of us (2 Corinthians 2:11). In other words, if you know how the enemy works, then it's easier to not allow him to take advantage of you.

One of the greatest tools that an army can use in a war is intelligence. They send spies out into the enemy's camp so they can know what the enemy's plan is. If they know how the enemy thinks and how the enemy attacks, then they can be prepared and defeat them when they come against them.

It is time for the body of Christ to recognize the source of attacks in their lives and take authority over the demons who are the cause. It is time to stop and say, "I take authority over you, in the name of Jesus and I command you to cease and desist. Get out of my path. I block you from my family. I plead the blood of Jesus over my family and you have no entrance here!" Take your God-given authority and use it!

Doctrines of Demons

Now the Spirit expressly says that in latter times some will depart from the faith, giving heed to deceiving spirits and doctrines of demons.

1 Timothy 4:1

Someone may ask, "What is it that a demon would teach?" The answer is quite simple. Anything that is opposed to, opposite of, or not in agreement with the Word of God has its foundation in the kingdom of darkness. The Word of God creates and brings life and the demonic teachings bring destruction and death.

However, this scripture in First Timothy tells us that in the last days there will be those who will act upon demonic instruction. That is happening in these days. In my youth, abortions, euthanasia, anti-Semitism, beheadings, and public mass executions were things that had mostly happened in the past, although from time to time we would hear of things like this happening. But today, we see they are daily current events. All of these atrocities are a result of people who listened to the doctrines of demons. Sadly, many of these teachings have been brought into acceptance in some major universities.

Their Judgment Is Sealed

So in these last days, it is imperative that every born-again believer know their authority over the forces of evil and not allow the deceptive lies of the evil one to cause you to pull back and withdraw. When you stand in faith and know and speak the Word of God by calling those things that be not as though they are, you will see the victory.

Remember 1 Corinthians 6:3 says there will be a day when the Church will stand in judgment over fallen angels. Their judgment has already been sealed and once proclaimed, they will be committed to eternal damnation in the lake of fire.

> *Then He will also say to those on the left hand, "Depart from Me, you cursed, into the everlasting fire prepared for the devil and his angels."*

> *Matthew 25:41*

> *The devil, who deceived them, was cast into the lake of fire and brimstone where the beast and the false prophet are. And they will be tormented day and night forever and ever.*

> *Revelation 20:10*

As Christians, we must understand that the battle we have with the realm of darkness is not a battle fought in the flesh. Second Corinthians 10:3 says, *"For though we walk in the flesh, we do not war according to the flesh."* The battle that we are in is a spiritual battle; however, the victory we receive on the spiritual battlefield will eventually be manifested in the physical realm. The victory in the realm of the unseen will become evident in the realm of the seen.

> *For the weapons of our warfare are not carnal but mighty in God for pulling down strongholds, casting down arguments and every high thing that exalts itself against the knowledge of God.*

> *1 Corinthians 10:4,5*

Chapter 5

The Garden of Eden

Many ancient cultures record the story of the first man and the first woman on earth. But with all these variations that are recorded in pagan cultures, the Bible clearly tells us of the true creation and purpose of man on the earth. On the sixth day, God created man and placed him in the Garden of Eden. In spite of the rebellion in Heaven, God's plan for man was progressing as scheduled.

The Earth Before Man

After Satan was cast down to the earth, the Bible does not mention Paradise being in Heaven until the New Testament. Of course, Heaven is mentioned; however, the specific place called the Paradise of God is not.

The Bible tells us that another reason Satan was cast down to the earth was because of his disproportionate trading and commerce (Ezekiel 28:16).

You traded with other nations and became more and more cruel and evil. So I forced you to leave my mountain, and the

*creature (guardian cherub) that had been your protector now
chased you away from the gems.*

Ezekiel 28:16 (CEV)

Since the Scriptures say that there was commerce, nations,
and kings before Satan was cast down, and since Scriptures tell us
Adam and Eve were not placed in the garden until after this, then
who was it that Satan was trading with and how could there be
commerce? Also, the Scriptures tell us that he was cast down before
kings who mocked him (Ezekiel 28:17). Who were these kings and
where were their kingdoms? These are questions asked by many
and sometimes the only answer we hear is, "I don't know," or "You
just aren't supposed to know these things."

However, there is one truth that I discovered years ago and it is
this: If it is in the Bible, it is not there to confuse or mislead us. It
is there for our knowledge and it is to be studied and learned. God
would never tell us something unless He wanted us to know it. With
that in mind, let's briefly examine what we know about this event.

First, angels were created before man and when Lucifer, who
was an angel, sinned and was cast out of Heaven, man had not yet
been placed in the Garden of Eden. However there was trading
and commerce of some type in existence and Lucifer was heavily
involved in it.

We know that Adam was the first man God created, so the
trading that Lucifer was involved in was with another intelligent
group of beings that at the very least, had something to trade with
Lucifer that he wanted. If it were not desired by Lucifer and if it

did not have some type of value, then there would not have been any reason to be deceitful in the business trades. These beings were grouped into nations and had kings. They obviously spoke, reasoned, and had intelligence. Who were they and where did they go?

They may have been angels or they may have been another creation of God because we know there are other heavenly hosts, but we know they were not men as we are today because Adam was the first man (1 Corinthians 15:45) and he was not created until after the fall of Lucifer. We also know that their number was great enough that they were divided into nations with kings. Nations have boundaries, laws, military, and currency. Obviously, there was a great civilization of some type and we know they were on the earth because Lucifer was cast down before them and he was cast to the earth.

The Bible doesn't tell us who they were, just that they were here. Someday all our questions will all be answered and it will probably be very soon. As we study the Holy Scriptures, the Holy Spirit will reveal the mysteries to us. The Holy Spirit is the Spirit of Truth.

The Word of God tells us what is important for us. The Bible doesn't give us all the history of eternity or very many details about eternity future, but it tells all we need to know for our creation and what pertains to us.

God's Original Plan

Man was placed by God in a garden eastward of Eden. He was to tend and keep it. It was Paradise, the Garden of God. The tree of life was there. The serpent (Satan) brought deception, the woman received the deception and the man and woman acted on it. Ultimately, the responsibility was on man because man was the one God instructed and he failed to obey.

God's original plan was for man to take dominion over all the earth, living eternally in harmony and fellowship with God, and being assisted by the angels of God. But because of the free will that God had given His creations, things did not go as designed. Because of the nature of God and His ability to see through the corridors of time without restriction, He adjusted His plan to fit man's failures.

From the foundation of the world, God knew that His Son would need to be the ultimate sacrifice to bring man back into line with God's eternal purpose for him (1 Peter 1:19-21). The grace and mercy of God far exceeds the imagination of man and through His grace and mercy, He has allowed man to repent and regain fellowship that was broken in the garden. Now let's take a look at how this all came about.

After the creation of the heavens and the earth, there was no vegetation on the earth and no plants had yet sprouted because there had been no rain upon the earth and because there was no man to cultivate the ground. However, there was a mist that would rise from the earth and water the whole surface of the ground. It was during this time that the Lord God formed man from the dust of the ground and into his nostrils He breathed the breath of life. This dust that had been formed into a man became a living being.

The Garden of Eden

Eastward of Eden

The Lord God planted a garden toward the east in Eden and He took the man that He had formed and placed him there. Then out of the ground vegetation began to grow and trees that yielded fruit good for food grew in abundance.

In this garden on the east side of Eden that God had planted, He also placed two trees – the tree of life and the tree of the knowledge of good and evil. Out of Eden, water flowed into the garden and as the water flowed from the garden east of Eden, it was divided and it became four rivers. The name of the first river was Pishon that flowed around the whole land of Havilah. In this area, there was gold and precious stones (bdellium and onyx). The second river of the four was Gihon, which flowed around the entire land of Cush. The third river was the Tigris (also called Hiddekel) that flowed east of Assyria. The fourth river was the Euphrates.

Then God placed man in the Garden of Eden for the purpose of cultivating and maintaining it. When He did this, He spoke to the man and told him that while he was there, he could eat freely of all the fruit that was available, except he was not to eat from the tree of the knowledge of good and evil and if he did, he would die that very day.

Adam Was Created Complete

I have had children ask me if Adam was created with a belly button (navel). Actually, I've had several adults ask me the same question. The answer is not given in Scripture. However, Adam was created complete in every way. He didn't have to grow hair, didn't have to grow teeth, and he had fingernails. He was created with all the features of a man that would have matured from birth, had he been born. He wasn't an oddity; he was created with all the intellect and features of an adult man. He was the human template which all mankind would follow.

I've also been asked what language Adam spoke and the answer to that is quite obvious to me. Since he conversed with God, he probably spoke Hebrew. When Jesus spoke from the light on the road to Damascus to Saul (Paul the apostle), the Bible tells us that He spoke in Hebrew (Acts 26:14). When Moses came down from Mt. Sinai and had the two tablets that had commandments written by the finger of God inscribed upon them, the tablets were inscribed in the Hebrew language (Exodus 31:18).

The Bible tells us that God does not change, thus He has not had a language shift. In Heaven, names are written on doors, books, and even on the foreheads of the saints. They are not written in English, French, German, or Arabic. They are written in the language of God. To think that Adam and God conversed in any other language would take a leap from logic and common sense.

The Creation of Woman

God said that man should not be alone and that he needed companionship that was suitable for him. God brought every beast of the field and bird that He had formed out of the ground to Adam to see what he would call them. Whatever he called the living creature, that became its name. And so as God brought the animals to Adam to be named, of course nothing was found that was comparable to him (Genesis 2:19,20).

God caused a deep sleep to come upon the man and God took a rib (Hebrew: *side*) from the man and fashioned it into a woman[1] (Genesis 2:22). God brought her and presented her to the man, and the man said, *"This is now bone of my bones and flesh of my flesh; she shall be called Woman* (Hebrew: *ishshah*) *because she was taken out of Man"* (Hebrew: *ish*) (Genesis 2:23). It was at this point that Adam and Eve became husband and wife (Genesis 2:24).

The Temptation

The Bible does not tell us how long the man and his wife, Adam and Eve, lived in the garden before the serpent (fallen Lucifer) showed up. But there was a day when Satan, taking the form of a serpent, approached the woman and confronted her with a question. He said to the woman, "Indeed has God said, 'You shall not eat from any tree of the garden?'" And the woman said to the serpent, "We may eat of the fruit of the trees of the garden. But the fruit of the tree which is in the middle of the garden, God said, 'You shall not eat from it or touch it lest you die.'" And the serpent said to the woman, "You will not die." Then he continued to reason with the woman and he said, "For God knows that in the day you eat of it, your eyes will be opened, and you will be like God, knowing good

[1]Rabbi Nosson Sherman, *The Chumash, The ArtScroll Series / Stone Edition* (Brooklyn, NY: Menorah Publications, Ltd., 2000), 14-15.

and evil" (Genesis 3:1-5, my paraphrase).

Several things happened in this conversation that should never have happened. The first mistake was listening to Satan. The second mistake was answering his question. And the third mistake was contemplating his reasoning, which leads to actions contrary to the Word of God.

In the same way faith and holiness increase through reading the Word of God and associating with the things of God, fear and deception increase by listening to the words of the devil and associating with evil people who are constantly promoting actions contrary to God's commands. This is exactly what happened to Eve. After listening to the words of the serpent, she saw that the tree was good for food and that it was pleasant to the eyes and desiring to be wise, she took fruit from the tree and ate it. Then she took the fruit to her husband, gave it to him, and he ate it. After their act of disobedience, their eyes were opened and they saw that they were naked, only now they were ashamed because of their nakedness. The glory that clothed them was gone and they attempted to cover themselves with fig leaves by sewing them together (Genesis 3:6,7).

The Sin of Adam

Although Adam and Eve both ate of the fruit (the Bible does not say it was an apple) and they both suffered the punishment of the disobedience, we are told that sin was brought into the world by one man's (Adam's) disobedience, but that the woman was deceived (Romans 5:19, 2 Corinthians 11:3).

I believe that when Eve brought the fruit to Adam, if Adam had been obedient to his instruction from God, there would have been no sin, even though Eve had been deceived. It was when Adam yielded to the temptation and ate the fruit that their sin was born. It was Adam who was told to not eat from the tree of the knowledge of good and evil in the midst of the garden. In fact, he was told this before Eve was created (Genesis 2:16,17), and it was his responsibility to instruct her in this restriction. However, when she told Satan that God had told them to not eat from that tree, she added to what God had said by saying that it could not even be touched (Genesis 3:3). Evidently, Adam instructed her poorly, or she did not listen carefully.

Since it was Adam's responsibility to know and obey God's command and to instruct his wife, I believe that if he would have corrected the one who was under his authority (Eve), they would not have been kicked out of the garden. Although Eve was deceived and fell into transgression (1 Timothy 2:14), Adam was the one that God had instructed and as a result, he was accountable. Adam had the authority to correct Eve, but he didn't.

Instead of enforcing the commandment of God, he yielded to the temptation that was brought on by Eve's deception. They both ate the fruit from the tree of the knowledge of good and evil that was in the midst of the garden which Adam's wife brought to him. The ultimate responsibility for the sin was on Adam's shoulders.

By not having faith in God's word to him, Adam displeased God (Hebrews 11:6). He was not obedient and that can be a lesson for all of us. If we are told not to do something, we should not rationalize. We must follow God's instruction in His Word. If we don't, the result could be devastating.

Who Said That?

After the deception of Eve and the sin of Adam, and after their attempt to cover themselves with fig leaves, they heard the sound of God walking in the garden in the cool of the day. They hid themselves among the trees of the garden so that God could not see them. Then God called the man and said, "Where are you?"

We must remember that God is all knowing and that He never asks a question that He doesn't already know the answer to. But He asks us questions in order to measure our heart through our response. The man replied by saying that he heard the Lord in the garden and was afraid to show himself because he was naked. When God heard this response, He said to the man, "Who told you that you were naked? Have you eaten from the tree that I commanded you not to eat?"

This reminds me of a time when I walked into my daughter's bedroom when she was only five years old. The room had been previously cleaned and everything had been put neatly away, but when I walked into the room, the room was a mess. Things had been pulled out of the drawers and blankets had been placed over chairs in order to make a play house. I looked through the door and asked her, "Who made this mess?" She looked at the floor and said, "I don't know." Her response was almost humorous because I knew full well that she was the only one who could have done it.

The Blame Game

When God said to Adam, "Who told you that you were naked?" God knew full well what had happened. But instead of the man taking responsibility for the command that he had been given, he shifted the blame to God and said, "The woman that You gave me, she gave me from the tree and I ate." The man was implying that if God had not given him the woman as a wife, then he wouldn't have sinned. His statement was clearly a result of pride.

Then the Lord God spoke to the woman and asked, "What have you done?" Likewise, she blamed it on the serpent and said, "I was deceived. The serpent is the one who deceived me, and I ate." Although she told the truth about the sin, that did not eliminate the sin.

Over the years I, like many people, have dealt with the issue of keeping my weight under control. I have had no one to blame for what I eat other than myself. Oh, I have tried to blame others. I have said that because it was the holidays, I ate. Sometimes I have said I was really hungry, so I ate. Sometimes I said I couldn't resist the desserts my family baked because they looked so good. But ultimately it was my hand that picked up the fork that put the food in my mouth. I had no one to blame but myself.

Likewise, Eve may have been deceived by the serpent, but by her own admission she is the one who ate the fruit.

The Curse

Then the Lord God said to the serpent, *"Because you have done this, you are cursed more than all cattle, and more than every beast of the field; on your belly you shall go, and you shall eat dust all the days of your life. And I will put enmity between you and the woman, and between your seed and her Seed; He shall bruise your head, and you shall bruise His heel"* (Genesis 3:14,15).

Then the Lord God turned to the woman and He spoke to her and said, *"I will greatly multiply your sorrow and your conception; in pain you shall bring forth children; your desire shall be for your husband, and he shall rule over you"* (Genesis 3:16).

Then after speaking to the woman, He spoke to Adam and He said, *"Because you have heeded the voice of your wife, and have eaten from the tree of which I commanded you, saying, 'You shall not eat of it': Cursed is the ground for your sake; in toil you shall eat of it all the days of your life"* (Genesis 3:17).

After God pronounced judgment on the serpent and Adam and Eve, He made garments of skin for Adam and his wife and He clothed them. This was the first blood covenant between God and man. You cannot remove the skin of an animal without blood and a life was given, a sacrifice was made, so that man could be covered.

Setting the Stage for Redemption

Then the Lord God said, *"'Behold, the man has become like one of Us, to know good and evil. And now, lest he put out his hand and take also of the tree of life, and eat, and live forever'— therefore the Lord God sent him out of the garden of Eden to till the ground from which he was taken"* (Genesis 3:22,23).

Here we see where the Father, the Word, and the Holy Spirit were in full agreement that Adam and Eve had to leave the Paradise of God, the garden eastward in Eden, because the Garden of God contained the tree of life and the sacrifice had not yet been made for man to have everlasting life. Had man eaten from the tree of life in his fallen state, he would have been condemned for eternity.

So God drove man out of the garden, and at the east of the Garden of Eden, He stationed cherubim and the flaming sword that would turn every direction to stand guard and prevent man from re-entering the garden and reaching the tree of life.

The Seed of the Woman

In Luke 8, Jesus told the parable about the sower. After He told the parable, His disciples came to Him and said, "What does this parable mean?" Jesus then answered in verse 11 with this unique statement. "Now the parable is this: The seed is the word of God."

We understand that the Seed of the woman in Genesis is Jesus. But could the verse also have another symbolic meaning? Could it be that the Seed of the woman and the seed of the serpent are words?

When the devil tempted Jesus and tried to deceive Him, Jesus responded with the Word of God (Luke 4:4-12). All three times when the devil tempted Jesus, Jesus spoke the Word. When Jesus quoted the written Word of God, Satan was powerless.

Jesus, who was the Seed of the woman, and Himself the Word of God, defeated the devil by using the Seed, which is the Word of God (John 1:14).

As Christians, we are to fight the forces of evil the same way Jesus did. We are to speak the Word. As believers, we are the children of God. That makes us offspring of God and His seed also. We are to speak His Word with power and authority. The result is we continue to bruise the head of the serpent daily by saying "It is written."

The Seed of the woman (the Word of God) always has and always will bruise the seed (the lying words) of the devil.

The Day Adam Died

God told Adam that on the day he ate of the tree of the knowledge of good and evil, that he would die that very day (Genesis 2:17). Many Bible students have wondered why Adam did not die within a 24-hour period after eating the fruit, but instead lived another 930 years (Genesis 5:5) and died just a little over 100 years before Noah was born. The answer here is explained by understanding God's timeline, that with God one day is as a thousand years and a thousand years is as a day (2 Peter 3:8). Adam didn't live through a full day on God's timetable.

The Trees in the Garden

When the Bible talks about the tree of life and the tree of the knowledge of good and evil, these are specific trees. There is one tree of life and one tree of the knowledge of good and evil. Every time that the tree of life is mentioned in the Word of God, it is in a place that is completely under the authority and control of God the Father. Anytime that sin is discovered in this place, the personality that is the source of the sin is cast out.

When iniquity was found in Lucifer in the Garden of God in Heaven, he was cast out. Likewise, when iniquity was found in Adam in the Garden of God eastward in Eden, he was cast out. The tree of life is holy unto the Lord and the unrighteous cannot partake of it. Two cherubim were placed on the ark of the covenant to symbolically protect the mercy seat. But real living cherubim were placed on the east side of the garden with a rotating flaming sword to protect the tree of life.

Those who receive Jesus as their Lord and Savior, who believe that He died for our sins, and that God raised Him from the dead, and publically confess with no denial that Jesus is Lord will be saved and allowed to eat the fruit from the tree of life that spans the crystal river in the New Jerusalem (Revelation 22:2,14). They will fulfill the mission of Jesus that was brought forth from the heart of Father God. Jesus explained it this way. He said, *"For God so loved the world that He sent His only begotten Son, that whoever would believe in Him should not perish but have everlasting life"* (John 3:16).

The Paradise of God

He who has an ear, let him hear what the Spirit says to the churches. To him who overcomes I will give to eat from the tree of life, which is in the midst of the Paradise of God.

Revelation 2:7

Chapter 6

Paradise in the Heart of the Earth

After Adam and Eve were driven out of the garden, the next mention of Paradise is in the heart of the earth. There in the heart of the earth were two compartments: Hades and Paradise (the bosom of Abraham). This area of the underworld continued as two compartments until the day that God raised Jesus from the dead (Romans 8:11). At that time, Paradise was emptied of all of its inhabitants, and after the resurrection of Jesus, they walked the streets of Jerusalem before ascending into the Paradise of God in the third Heaven (Matthew 27:52,53).

How do we know that Paradise was in the heart of the earth? This can simply be answered by briefly looking at three scriptures. In Matthew 12:40, Jesus said He was spending three days and three nights in the heart of the earth. In Ephesians 4:9-10, Paul said that before Jesus ascended, He descended. And in Luke 23:43, Jesus said that on the day of His crucifixion, He would be in Paradise.

The only possible way all three of these scriptures could be true would be that Jesus descended into Paradise in the heart of the earth. Because man rejected God, Paradise was moved into the heart of the earth. God did not desert man.

The Bosom of Abraham and Hades

From the fall of man until the resurrection of Jesus, there were two compartments in the heart of the earth. One compartment was Hades and the other compartment was the Paradise of God that is sometimes referred to as the bosom of Abraham.

After man was driven out of the Garden of Eden, there were those who followed God and those who did not. When they died, the spirits of those who rejected God (heathen, unrighteous) went to the compartment in the heart of the earth, Hades. Those who believed and trusted in God (righteous) went to the other compartment in the heart of the earth, the bosom of Abraham, which is called Paradise.

1 - The Bosom of Abraham

In the days of the Bible, men wore robes and in the chest area of the robe there was a lining that was called the bosom. In this lining, they kept their valuables as they traveled. In today's language, that would be akin to a woman's purse or a man's wallet. The bosom of Abraham was an illustrative term implying that it contained items of great value. Saying that Lazarus was in the bosom of Abraham was another way of saying that Lazarus was very valuable and kept in a safe place.

In Hebrews chapter 11, there are several Old Testament saints mentioned who were regarded as faithful. They were obviously in the bosom of Abraham comfortably waiting for the manifestation of the Messiah to come. Some of these Old Testament saints lived before the law of God was given to Moses on Mt. Sinai and some lived later under the law. This clearly tells us that Old Testament saints' admission to the bosom of Abraham was not determined by the law, but rather by their belief in or faith in God.

Rahab the harlot (prostitute) had done bad things, but because she honored God to the best of what she knew, Rahab was listed as one of the people of faith (Hebrews 11:31) and was an ancestor in the lineage of Jesus (Matthew 1:1,5). When she and the other saints listed in Hebrews 11 died, their spirits went to the bosom of Abraham. Some of those listed were before the law and some were not. Again, obedience to the law was not what determined a person's entry into Paradise. It was their faith in God and their obedience to His Word.

#2 - Hades

The other compartment is called Hades. It is the compartment where those who rejected God's Word (unrighteous) and opposed Him went when they died. When Jesus told the story of the rich man and Lazarus, this is where the rich man was. God never intended for man to be in hell separated from Him for all eternity. Hell was not created for the purpose of being a prison for man. It was created for the angels who rebelled against God in Heaven by following Lucifer in his rebellion.

*Then He will also say to those on the left hand, "Depart from
Me, you cursed, into the everlasting fire prepared for the devil
and his angels."*

Matthew 25:41

The Rich Man and Lazarus

In Luke's gospel, chapter 16, Jesus talked about two men who
experienced physical death. This was not a parable, but an actual
event that took place, because Jesus never used proper names in a
parable. When we examine what happened after the physical deaths
of these men, we can understand more about how we will be after
our physical bodies quit working in the time before we receive our
resurrected bodies.

Let's take a look at the story now exactly as Jesus told it to His
disciples as recorded in Luke 16.

*There was a certain rich man who was clothed in purple and
fine linen and fared sumptuously every day. But there was a
certain beggar named Lazarus, full of sores, who was laid at
his gate, desiring to be fed with the crumbs which fell from the
rich man's table. Moreover the dogs came and licked his sores.
So it was that the beggar died, and was carried by the angels
to Abraham's bosom. The rich man also died and was buried.
And being in torments in Hades, he lifted up his eyes and saw
Abraham afar off, and Lazarus in his bosom.*

*Then he cried and said, "Father Abraham, have mercy on
me, and send Lazarus that he may dip the tip of his finger in*

water and cool my tongue; for I am tormented in this flame."
But Abraham said, "Son, remember that in your lifetime you
received your good things, and likewise Lazarus evil things;
but now he is comforted and you are tormented. And besides
all this, between us and you there is a great gulf fixed, so that
those who want to pass from here to you cannot, nor can those
from there pass to us."

Then he said, "I beg you therefore, father, that you would send
him to my father's house, for I have five brothers, that he may
testify to them, lest they also come to this place of torment."
Abraham said to him, "They have Moses and the prophets; let
them hear them." And he said, "No, father Abraham; but if one
goes to them from the dead, they will repent." But he said to
him, "If they do not hear Moses and the prophets, neither will
they be persuaded though one rise from the dead."

Luke 16:19–31

This passage reveals a great number of things about hell, the bosom of Abraham, and life after death. Before we explore these details, we must fully understand that both people in this true event related by Jesus lived and died under the Old Covenant. The Church did not yet exist and salvation (the born-again experience) was not available at that time. This event occurred before the death, burial, and resurrection of Jesus while the departed Old Testament saints were all residing in the bosom of Abraham.

A biblical truth concerning the human spirit is this. The spirit of man must have a body in order to live on the earth. When the physical body dies, it stays on the earth and decays, but the spirit must go somewhere. At this point in time there were only two places available for the spirit to enter.

Let's take a moment and examine the hidden mysteries revealed in this passage.

1) **Riches did not determine their destination.**

It has been erroneously taught by many that the rich man went to Hades because he was rich, and that Lazarus went to the bosom of Abraham because he was poor. While prosperity is a blessing from God, there are those who are evil and have great wealth. Jesus was illustrating the reality that riches cannot buy you a place in the kingdom of God.

2) **Angels escort departed saints to Paradise.**

When Lazarus died, he was carried by multiple angels to Abraham's bosom (vs. 22).

3) **The unrighteous simply go to the grave.**

When the rich man died, he woke up and found himself in Hades.

4) **The unrighteous in Hades are tormented.**

Because the unrighteous are separated from God, there is no light or life. Darkness is the absence of light and death is the absence of life (John 8:12). God is light and life (John 1:4) and without Him, there is no peace. The death (absence from God) experienced in Hades is not a one- time experience in which a person ceases to exist, but is an eternal death without end. Likewise, the torment experienced is not just one torment or one type of torment but, according to Luke 16:23, is multiple torments.

5) **The unrighteous have senses and emotion.**

The rich man had sight, hearing, and could speak. His sight and conversation were not restricted to Hades. He could see over into the bosom of Abraham and could see that Lazarus had the ability to obtain water. The rich man had the desire to drink. Obviously, there was water flowing in Paradise and none in Hades. In fact, Hades had some type of flame that was tormenting the rich man.

Also, the man in Hades experienced the pain of regret from his past life, knowing that he had the choice to be in the bosom of Abraham and that he had chosen poorly. He also had the "burning desire" to keep his five brothers from going to Hades. He had enough mental ability to attempt to bargain with Abraham. He was told that no amount of begging would work and that nothing he could say would change things for those who were still alive.

Possibly one of the greatest torments would be knowing that you were confined for eternity separated from God while being able to see the righteous in comfort.

6) **There is peace for the righteous in Paradise.**

While the unrighteous were experiencing pain and could see into the bosom of Abraham, the righteous were experiencing comfort. By definition, comfort is a state of peace and contentment, exempt from stress and worry.

7) **Hades and Paradise are separated.**

Jesus clearly states in this event that there is a great gulf separating the bosom of Abraham and Hades and that the people from Hades cannot pass into Paradise, nor can those in Paradise pass into Hades. This signifies eternal security and eternal damnation.

Keep in mind this event happened under the Old Covenant and before Jesus put His blood on the Mercy Seat. Paradise was one of two compartments, along with Hades, in the depths of the earth.

Old Testament Saints

The spirits of the Old Testament saints were taken by angels to Paradise (the bosom of Abraham) when they died. Their bodies remained on the earth to return to dust (Genesis 3:19).

These Old Testament saints heard the victory preached by Jesus during His three days in the heart of the earth. After His resurrection, they came out of their graves and appeared to many in Jerusalem before going on to Heaven. No longer are they in the heart of the earth, but now they are a part of the great cloud of witnesses cheering on the Church (Hebrews 12:1). The spirits of these Old Testament saints now occupy the Paradise of God in Heaven which is a place of great comfort and joy (Psalm 16:11).

Daniel 12:1-2 prophesied that there would be a resurrection of God's people at the end of the Great Tribulation. Of course, he was prophesying to and talking about the Jews. This resurrection takes place at the same time as the resurrection of the tribulation saints who have been martyred for their faith.

Where Are They Now?

Now, the heart of the earth only contains the compartment of Hades and Hades contains the unrighteous dead. These imprisoned unrighteous dead will be resurrected and judged according to their works at the Great White Throne Judgment at the end of the Millennium (Revelation 20:5).

But Paradise, the tree of life, and the spirits of departed saints are now in Heaven. They are cheering on the Church on earth and eagerly awaiting the time when the Church will return with Jesus in the air at the Rapture and reclaim their resurrected bodies and then go to the Marriage Supper of the Lamb.

Chapter 7

The Death of Jesus and His Descent into Paradise

The Roman crucifixion was one of the most brutal and sadistic ways of execution recorded in history. After torturous scourging, which tore much of the flesh from the body of the person to be crucified, they were nailed and tied to a crossbar that was usually placed on a tree or post. Having been stripped naked, they were left in public view until death occurred. Many times birds and animals would eat of their bodies while they were still alive.

The Roman soldiers had developed methods that would inflict the greatest pain. The person being executed was nailed in such a way that their death would be prolonged in order to create unbearable agony until death. It's recorded that many times the only way that a breath could be taken would be for the one being crucified to push up with their feet, giving the rib cage room for a breath. But in their weakened state the crucified would then drop from the weight of their body, only to find they had to push themselves up again to gasp for another breath.

This is why the guards were going to break the legs of Jesus in order for Him to die before the Sabbath. However, after breaking the legs of both thieves on each side of Jesus, they found that Jesus' spirit had already left Him and they did not break His legs, thus fulfilling the prophecy that none of the Messiah's bones would be broken (John 19:36).

Two Thieves

When Jesus was crucified, there were two thieves also being crucified, one on each side of Him. The first thief ridiculed and rejected Jesus, but the second thief acknowledged Jesus as the Messiah. Jesus said to the second thief, *"Today you will be with me in Paradise"* (Luke 23:43).

For three hours there was darkness on the earth. Then at the ninth hour (3:00 p.m.), the veil of the temple was torn in two and Jesus cried out with a loud voice and said, *"Father, into Your hands I commit My spirit"* (Luke 23:46). As soon as He said this, He took His last breath. His body was taken off the cross and placed into a borrowed grave. However, the spirit of Jesus did not go to the grave with His body, but instead went into the heart of the earth as He had prophesied in Matthew 12:40.

It's interesting that Jesus did not tell the thief who honored Him, "Today after we both die, we will be together in Heaven," but rather Jesus told him that after their bodies died, they would be together in Paradise "today." After Jesus and the two thieves died from their crucifixion, Jesus and one thief went to Paradise, and the other thief went to Hades.

The Descent into the Heart of the Earth

For as Jonah was three days and three nights in the belly of the great fish, so will the Son of Man be three days and three nights in the heart of the earth.

Matthew 12:40

Earlier in His ministry while teaching His disciples, Jesus told them that in the same way Jonah was in the belly of the fish three days and three nights, He would also be in the heart of the earth three days and three nights. He was referring to the amount of time that His body would be in the grave and that He would be in the heart of the earth where the two compartments were located.

Now this, "He ascended"—what does it mean but that He also first descended into the lower parts of the earth? He who descended is also the One who ascended far above all the heavens, that He might fill all things.

Ephesians 4:9,10

Preaching to the Saints

At His death, Jesus entered the heart of the earth. During the next three days, He entered both compartments. When He first entered the compartment of Paradise on the day of His execution, He proclaimed victory to the righteous spirits who had been kept there in the bosom of Abraham. We know He went there first because He told the thief that they would be in Paradise that very day.

These all died in faith, not having received the promises, but having seen them afar off were assured of them, embraced them and confessed that they were strangers and pilgrims on the earth. For those who say such things declare plainly that they seek a homeland. And truly if they had called to mind that country from which they had come out, they would have had opportunity to return. But now they desire a better, that is, a heavenly country. Therefore God is not ashamed to be called their God, for He has prepared a city for them.

Hebrews 11:13-16

Jesus Preached to the Fallen Spirits

After proclaiming victory in Paradise, He entered the compartment of Hades and proclaimed His victory over the spirit of Death and the spirit of Hades. He made a public spectacle of Satan (Colossians 2:15), proclaimed His victory, and then the Father God Almighty resurrected Jesus from the grave so He could put His precious blood, the blood of the Lamb that was slain, on the altar in Heaven.

For Christ also suffered once for sins, the just for the unjust, that He might bring us to God, being put to death in the flesh but made alive by the Spirit, by whom also He went and preached to the spirits in prison, who formerly were disobedient, when once the Divine longsuffering waited in the days of Noah, while the ark was being prepared, in which a few, that is, eight souls, were saved through water.

1 Peter 3:18-20

There have been those who have interpreted these verses to say that it is possible for a person to have a second chance to receive Jesus after they have died. This is definitely a wrong interpretation of these verses. Jesus said, and many ancient Jewish writings confirm, that this text is specifically referencing angels who were imprisoned by God waiting for the fulfillment of their judgment. These are the same spirits that are mentioned in 2 Peter 2:4. At the time of Noah, these spirits were not spared and were committed to chains of darkness, reserved for judgment at the end of the Millennium.

The Keys of Death and Hell

Having disarmed principalities and powers, He made a public spectacle of them, triumphing over them in it.

Colossians 2:15

I am He who lives, and was dead, and behold, I am alive forevermore. Amen. And I have the keys of Hades and of Death.

Revelation 1:18

Centuries ago, it was proposed by theologians that the reason Jesus descended was to take the keys to hell and death from Satan. Because Revelation 1:18 says that Jesus has the keys, theologians tried to determine when He got the keys. The correct answer is, the keys have never been out of His possession. He is the Creator of all things and has never relinquished authority to Satan in any area. Satan appears to have authority only when man refuses to use his authority or is tricked by Satan into proclaiming what Satan wants through his words. Satan's words have no power until they are spoken by a man.

Throughout history, Jesus is the one who has defeated Satan, and in the prophetic future, He is the one who will proclaim Satan's defeat, forever proving His authority over the devil.

When Jesus descended into Hades, He did not need a key or permission to enter. And when He was ready to leave, He left. Only someone with the keys can do that. He has always had and will always have the keys of Hades and Death. In John 10:17-18, Jesus said that He had the authority to lay down His own life, and He also had the authority to take it up again.

The False Teaching of Purgatory

The existence of a place called purgatory is a doctrine held by many religions. They believe it is a place a person goes to after death where they suffer in order to be purified (or purged) of their sin. Through the suffering of the person in purgatory and through actions and gifts of the living for the dead, the time in purgatory is believed to be shortened. Throughout history, there have been many abuses with this teaching and the living have been enslaved physically and financially in order to aid the ones they love who have died.

The concept of the dead going to a place of suffering and punishment before going to a place of rest is a concept that predates Christianity and was a common belief of many pagan cultures dating back thousands of years.

The truth is purgatory does not exist. A person's destiny after death is determined before death and according to Scripture, at death a person's spirit goes either to Hades or to the presence of the Lord. Jesus told us that there was a divide between the unrighteous dead and the righteous dead and that there was no crossing that barrier in either direction. There is the kingdom of darkness and the kingdom of light. There is not a kingdom of shadow in between.

Our eternal destiny is determined by our acceptance or rejection of Jesus Christ as Lord while we are living. Jesus said there was only one way to the Father and that was through Him (John 14:6). He paid the price in full and any additional price that anyone tries to pay is implying that the price Jesus paid was not enough. We are made righteous because of His blood sacrifice alone, and not by any sacrifice or purging that man can do.

Between the abode of the saints and the abode of the damned is a great gulf that is "fixed" (Luke 16:26). Those who are Christians are sealed by the Holy Spirit and no demon can break the seal that God establishes.

In whom also, having believed, you were sealed with the Holy Spirit of promise, who is the guarantee of our inheritance until the redemption of the purchased possession.

Ephesians 1:13,14

Purgatory does not exist and is a complete fabrication based in paganism.

For by grace you have been saved through faith, and that not of yourselves; it is the gift of God.

Ephesians 2:8

The Victory Lap

I live in the state of Missouri and every year our state has a state fair in the city of Sedalia. One of the main events is the stock car races. Professionals bring their vehicles and they race to the finish. When the checkered flag comes down and the winner is determined, the tradition is the winner circles the entire race track by himself in what is called the winner's victory lap.

When Jesus preached victory to the Old Testament saints in Paradise in the heart of the earth, it was a type of victory lap. The long-awaited good news had finally arrived and the promise of the Messiah had been fulfilled.

And then having drawn the sting of all the powers ranged against us, He exposed them, shattered, empty and defeated, in His final glorious triumphant act!

Colossians 2:15 (Phillips)

After the victory lap at the state fair, the winner steps onto the platform and receives his trophy and he is established as the victor.

When Jesus said, *"It is finished"* while on the cross, He had completed the race. Victory was His and the only thing left was to take His victory lap in Paradise and ascend into Heaven and place His blood on the altar, proclaiming His victory to the universe.

His trophy is currently being perfected and will be presented to Him without spot or blemish at the great wedding celebration shortly after the Rapture of the Church (Ephesians 5:27).

The Paradise of God

Chapter 8

His Victorious Resurrection

During His ministry, Jesus had a close friend, Lazarus, who had two sisters – Mary and Martha. Lazarus died and was buried, and it was four days after his death before Jesus arrived at the house of Mary and Martha. The Bible gives a miraculous account of how Jesus raised Lazarus from the dead.

While Jesus was at the tomb shortly before Lazarus came back to life, Martha told Jesus that she believed that there would be a day that Lazarus would rise again (John 11:24). But Jesus made a very profound statement to her. He said, *"I am the resurrection and the life"* (John 11:25).

I Am the Resurrection

The resurrection is not just an event. The resurrection is a person. Jesus is the resurrection.

After Jesus preached victory to the spirits of the saints in the bosom of Abraham (including the thief on the cross), and then proclaimed victory to the spirits in Hades, the power of God raised Him from the dead.

It should be no surprise to anyone that when His physical body was brought back to life by the Father and His spirit re-entered it as He came out of the grave, He brought with Him many of the saints from the bosom of Abraham. The resurrected saints who had been waiting in the bosom of Abraham entered Paradise in Heaven where Jesus put His blood on the altar and became the firstfruits, the firstborn, and the head of the body known as the Church.

> *At that moment the curtain of the temple was torn in two from top to bottom. The earth shook, the rocks split and the tombs broke open. The bodies of many holy people who had died were raised to life. They came out of the tombs after Jesus' resurrection and went into the holy city and appeared to many people.*
>
> *Matthew 27:51–53 (NIV)*

His Ascension into Heaven

The saints who followed Jesus evidently stayed in Heaven, but Jesus returned to the earth in His glorified body for forty days. He spent this time teaching and receiving into the Church all who believed and confessed that He was Lord.

Although Jesus was on the earth for forty days in His glorified body, He was not in His glorified body immediately after His resurrection. When the woman (Mary) approached Him at the tomb, Jesus told her she could not touch Him because He had not yet ascended and had not yet been glorified. But we know that later that day He invited the disciples to touch Him.

Jesus saith unto her, "Touch me not; for I am not yet ascended to my Father: but go to my brethren, and say unto them, I ascend unto my Father, and your Father; and to my God, and your God."

John 20:17 (KJV)

Now as they said these things, Jesus himself stood in the midst of them, and said to them, "Peace to you." But they were terrified and frightened, and supposed they had seen a spirit. And He said to them, "Why are you troubled? And why do doubts arise in your hearts? Behold My hands and My feet, that it is I Myself. Handle Me and see, for a spirit does not have flesh and bones as you see I have."

Luke 24:36-39

Evidently, a dramatic event took place in Heaven that changed Jesus in such a way that He moved from being untouchable to touchable. A dramatic shift in covenants, the beginning of the Last Days, and the start of the Church all started at this pinpoint, pivotal event that took place in Heaven.

The Most Important Day in History

He indeed was foreordained before the foundation of the world, but was manifest in these last times for you who through Him believe in God, who raised Him from the dead and gave Him glory, so that your faith and hope are in God.

1 Peter 1:20,21

The most important day in all of the history of man, the one day that changed everything for all eternity was the day that Jesus entered into Heaven and put His perfect blood on the altar and changed the destiny of humanity for all eternity.

First Peter 1:20 says that before the foundation of the world, Jesus was foreordained and destined to be the salvation of man. That means that even before creation in Genesis, God appointed Jesus to put His blood on the altar for our sins.

Of course, God did not cause Satan to rebel and God did not cause man to sin, but He foreknew the iniquity that would be found in them and He knew this before the foundation of the world. When He created man and put him in the garden, He knew the end from the beginning. Once again, God didn't cause it to happen, but God foreknew that it would happen.

This concept is not comprehendible in the limited mind of man, but in the unlimited mind of God who created time itself, it's natural. This is why when we place our trust in Him and rest in the knowledge that God has already seen tomorrow and has a plan, we can know it will be better than today, so we can be at peace today.

The Ark of the Covenant

For Christ has not entered the holy places made with hands, which are copies of the true, but into heaven itself, now to appear in the presence of God for us.

Hebrews 9:24

When God raised Jesus from the dead and He walked out of the tomb, we know that Mary was at the grave site. There He told her to not touch Him because He had not yet ascended unto the Father and He had not yet been glorified. As she left to tell the disciples, He ascended into Heaven into the Holy of Holies and He stood in front of the Ark of the Covenant (Hebrews 9:12).

You may remember that as the Israelites went into battle, many times they carried the Ark of the Covenant with them. The Ark of the Covenant was a golden box with the image of two angels on top of it with their wings outstretched covering the lid of the Ark of the Covenant, which was also named the Mercy Seat. This golden box contained the Ten Commandments on the tablets that were given to Moses when he came down from Mt. Sinai, the golden pot that had the manna, and Aaron's rod that produced many miracles (Hebrews 9:4). The Israelites were instructed not to touch the Ark of the Covenant. Once while transporting the Ark, it was touched and the man who touched it immediately died (2 Samuel 6:7).

However, when Jesus was in Heaven standing before the Ark of the Covenant, it was not the one the Israelites carried into battle and placed in the temple on earth. The Bible clearly tells us that one was a copy.

There are priests who offer the gifts according to the law; who serve the copy and shadow of the heavenly things, as Moses was divinely instructed when he was about to make the tabernacle. For He said, "See that you make all things according to the pattern shown you on the mountain."

Hebrews 8:4,5

The Ark of the Covenant that was in Heaven was the original that had been shown to Moses during the forty days he was on Mt. Sinai. Every year on the Day of Atonement (Yom Kippur) the high priest on earth would go into the holy of holies. While speaking the name of God twenty-six times, he would place the blood of an animal on the lid of the Ark of the Covenant (Mercy Seat) for the atoning or covering of the sins of the people. This the high priest would do year after year.

But the Ark that Jesus stood in front of in Heaven had never had blood placed on it before in all of eternity. It had been waiting for the perfect blood of the Lamb of God, for the once-and-for-all sacrifice that provided for the total remission of all sin.

Before Jesus placed His blood on the altar, the covenant that God had with man was the Law. But after Jesus placed His blood on the lid of the Ark of the Covenant, man was under the New Covenant of grace. When the blood of Jesus touched the Mercy Seat, old things passed away, all things became new. He received His glorified body and we received the promise of salvation that the Old Testament saints had looked forward to (Hebrews 11:13).

Precious Blood

Although Jesus was the Son of God, He continually proclaimed that He was the Son of Man. In order for His blood to redeem mankind, two things must have been present. First, it had to be the blood of a man and secondly, it had to be unspotted, untarnished, pure blood.

Of course, Jesus fulfilled the first part by being born of Mary, a virgin girl, who had never been with a man. Medical science tells us that the bloodline comes from the man. This is why in determining the father of a child, they check the blood of the father. The Bible tells us that the Holy Spirit of God came upon Mary and that she received the seed of God, conceived, and bore a child, Jesus.

Because Adam had sinned in the garden and was no longer clothed with the glory of God, his blood, and all of his descendants' blood, contained death. But the bloodline of Jesus was from His Father God and it contained life. So we can see that Jesus fulfilled the requirement of being a man and having pure blood. When He put His blood on the altar in Heaven, He became the perfect Lamb that was slain, the firstfruits in the kingdom, the firstborn among many brethren and spiritually took His place as the head of the Church and established it at that moment.

When He returned to earth later that day, He told His disciples to touch Him and handle Him and see that He was flesh and bone. (Luke 24:39). Why could they now touch Him? Because He had been glorified. Why did He say that He was flesh and bone? It's because His precious blood was on the altar in Heaven and the price for the redemption of man had been paid.

The Birth of the Church

Every person from that moment on who believed that Jesus Christ was the Son of God and that God raised Him from the dead and confessed it with their mouth, was saved and became a part of the Church.

If you confess with your mouth the Lord Jesus and believe in your heart that God has raised Him from the dead, you will be saved. For with the heart one believes unto righteousness, and with the mouth confession is made unto salvation. For the Scripture says, "Whoever believes on Him will not be put to shame."

Roman 10:9-11

Jesus taught for forty days and then made His final ascension into Heaven as recorded in the first chapter of Acts.

Jesus became the once-and-for-all sacrifice for sin. After His sacrifice, any person who received Jesus as their Lord and Savior was made righteous because of what He had done and not because of their own works.

Not that He should offer himself often, as the high priest enters the Most Holy Place every year with blood of another— He then would have had to suffer often since the foundation of the world; but now, once at the end of the ages, He has appeared to put away sin by the sacrifice of himself.

Hebrews 9:25,26

First John 1:7 says, *"But if we walk in the light as He is in the light, we have fellowship with one another, and the blood of Jesus Christ His Son cleanses us from all sin."* As Christians, we are cleansed from all sin, all unrighteousness has been removed, and although we must continually increase in our holiness and turn away (repent) from sins of the flesh, our spirit is eternally righteous and cleansed from all sin because of the blood that Jesus placed on the altar in Heaven the day of His resurrection.

For it is not possible that the blood of bulls and goats could take away sins.

Hebrews 10:4

By one man (Adam), the curse was brought into the earth and by another man (Jesus, the Son of God), sin was removed. Although the curse of the law was upon the nation of Israel, many Christians, through wrong teaching, have placed themselves under the curse. But the blood of Jesus has redeemed all mankind from the curse of the law.

Christ has redeemed us from the curse of the law, having become a curse for us (for it is written, "Cursed is everyone who hangs on a tree").

Galatians 3:13

The Glorified, Resurrected Body of Jesus

The glorified, resurrected body of Jesus is the template of the body every born-again believer will have throughout eternity. We have several scriptures that describe His body and give great insight to the way we will be forever. First of all, He appeared to have the body of a natural man. We know this because when Mary saw Him at the tomb, she thought He was the gardener. He didn't look like an angel. He didn't glow. Evidently there didn't seem to be anything odd about Him. He appeared to be a normal man going about His normal duties.

But although He appeared to have the features and characteristics of a normal man, there were many supernatural aspects to His body. We know that when He wanted to be inside of a room, that it was not necessary for there to be a door, because He appeared inside a room (John 20:26).

He appeared to be a natural man when He appeared to the two men who were walking on the road to Emmaus (Luke 24:15-16). He prepared fish and ate fish with Peter, but while He was talking with His disciples on the 40th day after His resurrection, He began floating up into the sky and slowly disappeared into Heaven while He was talking to them (Acts 1:9-11). His body operated beyond the natural laws of physics and was not governed by the rules of the universe (gravity).

For every Christian, this is good news. Jesus' resurrection guarantees your resurrection. Because of His blood sacrifice, Christians will forever have glorified bodies that live free from disease and death, with the ability to live in the Heavenly Jerusalem and the New Jerusalem, and travel at the speed of thought. As a Christian, your best days are truly ahead of you!

Chapter 9

Paradise in Heaven

He who has an ear, let him hear what the Spirit says to the churches. To him who overcomes I will give to eat from the tree of life, which is in the midst of the Paradise of God.

Revelation 2:7

After the resurrection of Jesus, Paradise is never again mentioned in Scripture as being in the heart of the earth.

The revelation of John, which is actually the revelation of Jesus Christ, says that when John had his vision of Heaven, he saw the tree of life in the Paradise of God in Heaven. That's where Paradise is now. Paradise is and will remain forever in Heaven.

There are people who say Heaven is just a metaphor for goodness and hell is just a metaphor for evil. No, there is a Heaven, there is a hell, and within Heaven there is a place called Paradise.

As a teenager, I attended high school in Raytown, Missouri. My family lived in the city of Raytown, which is located in the state of Missouri. Raytown is in Missouri, but it is not all of Missouri. In other words, I could travel from one side of the city of Raytown to the other side of the city and I would always be in Missouri. But on the other hand, I could travel from the western border of Missouri to the eastern border of Missouri and never be in Raytown.

Likewise, the Paradise of God is in Heaven. It is not all of Heaven, but a portion of Heaven. It's not a concept, it is a place. You can't be in the Garden of God without being in Heaven, but you can be in Heaven and not be in the Garden of God.

The Tree of Life

In the middle of its street, and on either side of the river, was the tree of life, which bore twelve fruits, each tree yielding its fruit every month. The leaves of the tree were for the healing of the nations.

Revelation 22:2

Within that portion of Heaven called the Paradise of God or the Garden of God is a tree called the tree of life. This is a specific tree and its leaves are life-giving. It is "the" tree of life, not "a" tree of life. In the Bible, this tree was first mentioned in the garden that God planted east of Eden. But now, the tree of life is in Heaven in God's garden.

You may remember that when God drove Adam out of the garden, He placed cherubim on the east side of the Garden of Eden and also He placed there a flaming sword which turned every way. He did this to guard the way specifically to the tree of life (Genesis 3:24).

However, now we find no mention of the tree being guarded. Why? Because it is in Heaven and only the righteous are in Heaven.

God has promised us in His Word that to everyone who overcomes, He will give them the opportunity to eat from the tree of life that is currently in the midst of the Paradise of God.

Blessed are those who do His commandments, that they may have the right to the tree of life, and may enter through the gates into the city.

Revelation 22:14

The tree is mighty in size and in its abundance of life-giving leaves. We know that in the New Jerusalem, this tree will be so large that it will span either side of the crystal river. It will be so magnificent that it will bear twelve different fruits, yielding its fruit every month. The leaves on the tree of life will produce the healing of the nations.

Comfort and Peace

While the tree of life is in the Garden of God (Paradise) in Heaven, it is not the only thing in the garden. The very context of the word "garden" or "orchard" denotes a place of comfort, peace, and pleasure. While the tree of life gives life through its fruit, there must also be other trees. An orchard would not be an orchard with only one tree. So, other trees must be there yielding other types of fruit.

Also, there are many other comforts. Remember when Lazarus was in Paradise under the earth, he was being comforted. Now, Paradise is a much more glorious place and the comforts are surely increased. In the Paradise that was called the bosom of Abraham, Jesus only visited for three days, but in the Paradise of Heaven, Jesus resides in the city that holds Paradise.

Residents of Paradise

Currently, the righteous spirits of men and women reside in Paradise with Jesus. These saints are one of two groups. The first group is the saints (people) who physically died before the sacrifice of Jesus who believed God by faith, looking forward to the promise. They were formerly in the bosom of Abraham.

The second group is made up of saints (people) who accepted Jesus as their Lord and Savior while they were living on the earth. They, of course, would have done this after He placed His blood on the mercy seat in Heaven on the day of His resurrection. This group is the Church. Their spirits stay there until Jesus returns in the Rapture.

Scripture clearly shows that when Jesus returns in the Rapture, that the spirits of all of the Christians in Heaven (those who sleep in Jesus), will return in the sky with Him. When Jesus appears in the sky with the New Testament saints from Paradise, the physical bodies of these saints will be resurrected from the ground and meet them in the air. After being accompanied by the raptured living saints, together they will all receive their glorified, resurrected bodies. That brings us to this question. What kind of bodies do the saints in Paradise have <u>before</u> they will receive their glorified, resurrected bodies?

The saints waiting in Heaven who have not yet received their glorified, resurrected bodies have a spiritual body. While not flesh and bone, it is still subject to comforts. They are able to think, remember, communicate, and have mobility, although restricted, until the Rapture where they receive an upgraded body.

John's Heavenly Guide

In John's vision of the Revelation of Jesus Christ, twice he begins to fall at the feet of his heavenly guide and is rebuked by his guide. He is told that he should not worship the guide but instead should worship God.

And I fell at his feet to worship him. But he said to me, "See that you do not do that! I am your fellow servant, and of your brethren who have the testimony of Jesus. Worship God! For the testimony of Jesus is the spirit of prophecy."

Revelation 19:10

The Greek word for angel (*angelos*) is spelled in Greek letters: *alpha gamma gamma epsilon lambda omicron sigma.* It is the word used and translated as *angel* in New Testament Greek. However, the word itself is not a translation but a transliteration. Let me explain.

To translate a word from one language to another, you take the meaning of the word from one language and translate that meaning into the writing of the second language. To transliterate a word means that you take the word in the original language and simply convert the letters of the word to the closest English letter available. This word *angelos* in New Testament Greek is transliterated in most texts and only translated in a few.

If we transliterate the word *angelos,* we take the first letter *alpha* and convert it to an "*a*". We take the next two letters which are *gamma gamma* and in the Greek, they have an *ng* sound when placed together. So we convert these two letters into the English counterpart of "*ng*". Then comes *epsilon* which is transliterated "*e*". Then the *lambda* is converted to an "*l*" and the *omicron sigma* is converted to an "s". This gives us the English word *angels.*

But if we translate the Greek word *angelos* into English, it means messenger. If you look up the definition of *angelos* in a biblical Greek to English dictionary, it will say "a messenger, envoy, one who is sent, an angel, a messenger from God."

Of course, in the New Testament, angels are messengers in most cases. They bring a message from God to the born-again saints and usually these messengers are spiritual angelic beings of great power. Such a messenger appeared to Peter in prison (Acts 12:7; Acts 5:19), to Phillip and told him to arise and go to the road from Jerusalem to Gaza (Acts 8:26), to the woman at the tomb of Jesus (John 20:12), and many others.

However, in John's revelation, this messenger was not an angelic being, but according to Revelation 22:9, he says that he was a fellow servant, that he was of the brethren, which meant he was human, and that he was a prophet. Which godly prophet was this? We are not told, but we do know this. John's guide was not a spiritual angelic being like the ones who appeared and heralded the birth of Jesus, but rather he was one of John's brethren who was a prophet.

*Now I, John, saw and heard these things. And when I heard and saw, I fell down to worship before the feet of the angel (*messenger*) who showed me these things. Then he said to me, "See that you do not do that. For I am your fellow servant, and of your brethren the prophets, and of those who keep the words of this book. Worship God."*

Revelation 22:8,9

Thomas Nelson's recent translation (*The Voice*) shows this correction: *"I, John, am the one who heard and witnessed these visions. And when I heard and witnessed them, I fell prostrate at the feet of the **heavenly guide** who showed them to me"* (Revelation 22:8).

So why is it important to us to know that John's guide in Heaven was human? It lets us know that there are righteous beings who are not angels, but who were formerly on the earth and are functioning in Heaven now.

A Christian Never Dies

Remember, the real you is spirit. You are your spirit. Your spirit is you. The spirit of God is God. The spirit of Larry is Larry. When your body quits working, you leave your body here and you literally go to another place. The Bible says you are with the Lord and that place that you go to be with Him is in Heaven. Paul didn't say that at death, part of you stays here and part of you goes to Heaven. No, he said that when your body dies that you leave it and you go to be with the Lord. The old container died and will be resurrected and upgraded and you will again inhabit it.

A Christian never dies. When you accept Jesus as Lord, old things pass away and all things become new. Your spirit is reborn and you are now dead to sin. Spiritual death is no longer in your future, it is in your past. You don't die, your body does. It's just the container, the earthly temple, that dies. You (your spirit) move to a different place. It would be more proper to say that your physical body dies (and decays) and you depart (and never decay).

What Happens to a Christian when Their Body Dies?

1. The body ceases to function and can no longer contain a spirit (James 2:26).

2. The spirit leaves the body and is escorted by angels to the presence of the Lord, where all the joys and comforts of being in glory, seeing Jesus, and fellowship with all the departed saints will be enjoyed.

3. When the Lord Jesus returns to earth and appears in the sky (Rapture), your dead body will be resurrected and caught up into the air.

4. At the Rapture, your body will be upgraded to a glorified, resurrected body and you will forever inhabit your new body which is like the body that Jesus has.

5. After the Rapture, you will return to Heaven for seven years with the Lord in your newly glorified, resurrected body, where you will receive your rewards at the Judgment Seat of Christ and be in the Marriage Supper of the Lamb.

6. At the end of the seven years you will actually come to the earth with Christ out of Heaven and rule and reign with Him for one thousand years in the Millennial Kingdom.

7. After the one thousand years, there will be a New Jerusalem that will be your home for all eternity.

8. You will have individuality because you will be given a name that only He knows (Revelation 2:17), and you will have His name on your forehead. He is yours and you are His.

The Passageway to Paradise

But I do not want you to be ignorant, brethren, concerning those who have fallen asleep, lest you sorrow as others who have no hope. For if we believe that Jesus died and rose again, even so God will bring with Him those who sleep in Jesus.

1 Thessalonians 4:13–14

"*But I do not want you to be ignorant, brethren...*" The root word of the word "ignorant" is ignore. You can be ignorant about a specific subject because you don't study it, and just ignore it. There are highly intelligent people who go to church who don't know anything about the Rapture because they ignore it. Paul tells us that he does not want us to ignore what happens to people who have "fallen asleep" (talking about those who have passed away) so that we will not sorrow as others who have no hope. In other words he is saying, "You should not be ignorant about life after death like the people of the world who do not know the Holy Scriptures."

My father was a good man. He was an ordained Southern Baptist deacon. He had lived a full life when he departed for Heaven. Did I sorrow when my dad died? Of course I did, but not like the world sorrows when they experience death in their families.

When you know Jesus and you know His Word, you not only have hope, but a confident knowing that the goodbye on earth was not a final goodbye. It is separation for a while, but you know that eventually we will receive our new bodies that will never age or decay, and there will be a reunion with our loved ones. Our love and friendship will last for eternity.

The people of the world who do not know Jesus as Lord only have the fables of man and a false hope. Deep inside their spirits, they know their hope is futile and without substance.

We, on the other hand, have a substance called faith (Hebrews 11:1) that brings us through the valley of the shadow of death. For the Christian, the shadow cannot hurt us. The shadow of a weapon never hurt anyone. Death is nothing more than a shadow to a believer and the passageway into the Paradise of God in Heaven.

Chapter 10

Paul in Paradise

As a pastor, I have been with countless people as their spirits left their bodies. Even though the remaining family members knew that their loved one had departed to glory, there was sorrow because they knew they would not be able to fellowship with their friend or family member on this side of glory again. We all enjoy the companionship and fellowship of friends and family, and to have one depart can bring sorrow.

But the Bible tells us that we do not sorrow in the same way that the world sorrows because we know it's just a matter of time until we will be together again (1 Thesselonains 4:13). Unless you've actually been to glory like Paul the apostle however, it's almost impossible to grasp the awesome joy and excitement that exists in the Paradise of God.

I have heard people talk about how much they are looking forward to someday being in Heaven, but then they panic if they think something is going to get them there too soon. I understand it is difficult to long to go to a place where you've never been. While we know we experience victories in this life, it is hard to imagine what living in Heaven will be like without having a resurrected body yet.

Remember, when a Christian departs this life, it's only their spirit that goes to Heaven, and their body returns to the dust of the ground. While we know we will receive our glorified bodies at the Rapture, few realize the awesomeness of Heaven, even without a physical body. This is where we must look at what Paul, who had been in both places, tells us.

Paul had a beautiful experience. He was taken into a part of Heaven called Paradise. The word "paradise" in the Hebrew and in the Greek means "orchard or garden." He was literally taken to the Garden of God in Heaven. But how did this happen? What was the event that allowed him to enter? By his own words, he said that this event took place fourteen years before he wrote the letter to the church in Corinth (2 Corinthians 12:2). Where was he fourteen years earlier?

Paul, the Missionary

On Paul's first two missionary trips, he traveled to Lystra. Lystra is an ancient Greek city in the country that is now known as Turkey. It is mentioned six times in the New Testament and visited several times by the Apostle Paul, Barnabas, and Silas. It was there that Paul met a young disciple named Timothy (Acts 16:1,2).

The Roman Empire made Lystra a colony 600 years before Paul's visit and by the time Paul traveled there, it had been incorporated into the Roman province known as Galatia. Paul visited Lystra on his first missionary trip eighteen years after the crucifixion of Jesus and again two years later on his second missionary trip.

Acts 13 recounts Paul's first missionary journey. While Paul was in Antioch, he was separated by the Holy Spirit, along with Barnabas, for the work of the gospel. After the brethren had fasted and prayed, and laid hands on them, they sent them out to Seleucia and then from there, they sailed to Cyprus. When they arrived in Salamis, they preached in the synagogues and John assisted them.

They traveled on to the island of Paphos, where there was a Jewish false prophet and sorcerer whose name was Bar-Jesus, who was with the proconsul of the city. The proconsul called for Barnabas and Saul, because he wanted to hear the Word of God. But the sorcerer tried to turn the proconsul away from the faith. When Paul encountered him, he was not shy or timid, but rather looked intently at him and openly proclaimed, *"O full of all deceit and all fraud, you son of the devil, you enemy of all righteousness, will you not cease perverting the straight ways of the Lord? And now, indeed, the hand of the Lord is upon you, and you shall be blind, not seeing the sun for a time"* (Acts 13:10-11). Immediately a dark mist fell on Bar-Jesus and he was blinded. Because of that, the proconsul believed and Paul's fame spread across the region.

Then Paul and Barnabas sailed to Perga, which is located in Pamphylia. There, John left the group and returned to Jerusalem. After leaving Perga, they came to Antioch and went to the synagogue on the Sabbath day where the rulers of the synagogue read the law and the prophets. The synagogue rulers asked Paul to speak, so Paul stood up and with great gestures spoke boldly and delivered a powerful message. It was so well received that the Gentiles begged him to preach the message again to them on the next Sabbath.

On the next Sabbath, nearly the entire city came together to hear the Word of God spoken by the Apostle Paul. But with this great success came equally great envy among some of the prominent people and they opposed the things Paul was speaking. They stirred up the leaders of the city and Paul and Barnabas were persecuted and expelled from the region. But they shook the dust from their feet and went to Iconium where the disciples were filled with joy and filled with the Holy Spirit.

In Iconium, great multitudes of both the Jews and the Gentiles believed the gospel. But the unbelieving Jews stirred up the Gentiles and poisoned their minds toward Paul. So the city became divided into two groups. One group sided with the unbelieving Jews and the other group sided with the apostles. Violence broke out and word spread that Paul and Barnabas were going to be stoned. But Paul discovered this plot so they fled to Lystra.

The City of Lystra

In Lystra, great healings took place. But the town was full of idolatry; the people thought the missionaries were gods because of the great healings. They called Barnabas "Zeus" and Paul they called "Hermes." In the front of the city was the temple of Zeus and their priests brought sacrificial animals to the gates intending to sacrifice them to their new "gods."

When Paul and Barnabas heard this, they tore their clothes and ran among the multitudes of the people asking them why they were doing these things. They told them they needed to turn away from these useless practices, and turn to the living God who made Heaven and earth. But the more they preached, the more the multitudes wanted to sacrifice to them, calling them Zeus and Hermes.

The angry Jews from Antioch and Iconium then came to Lystra to persuade the multitudes to stone Paul. And so, the multitude picked up rocks and hurled them at Paul until he was dead. As they would do with any dead animal or unworthy person, they drug his body outside the city and left it to the animals or to decay.

Left for Dead

Everyone present believed that Paul was deceased. But his faithful disciples gathered around him and he rose up. Paul was not a man of fear because he immediately went back into the city to the people who thought they had killed him.

Then Jews from Antioch and Iconium came there (Lystra); and having persuaded the multitudes, they stoned Paul and dragged him out of the city, supposing him to be dead. However, when the disciples gathered around him, he rose up and went into the city. And the next day he departed with Barnabas to Derby.

Acts 14:19,20

I believe that from the moment Paul was stoned inside the city (and thought to be dead) until the time the disciples surrounded him and he miraculously rose up, that Paul was in Heaven itself and more specifically, went into the area called the Paradise of God.

Fourteen years after this, Paul wrote a letter to the church in Corinth telling them about an event that took place fourteen years earlier. Fourteen years earlier was when he was in Lystra, stoned and left for dead.

The Vision of Paradise

Paul said in his letter that fourteen years ago, he was caught up into the third heaven. He went on to say that he didn't understand exactly how it happened. He did not know whether he was in his body or out of his body. But this he did know. He went into the third heaven and in the third heaven he entered into Paradise and he was told things that earthly words were not capable of explaining.

It is doubtless not profitable for me to boast. I will come to visions and revelations of the Lord: I know a man in Christ who fourteen years ago—whether in the body I do not know, or whether out of the body I do not know, God knows—such a one was caught up to the third heaven. And I know such a man—whether in the body or out of the body I do not know, God knows— how he was caught up into Paradise and heard inexpressible words, which it is not lawful for a man to utter.

2 Corinthians 12:1-4

Remember, the thief on the cross (who acknowledged Jesus as Lord) immediately went to Paradise upon his death (Luke 23:43).

And we know that Lazarus was carried by the angels immediately upon his death to the bosom of Abraham (Paradise) (Luke 16:22). Paul said that when a person is absent from the body, they are present with the Lord (2 Corinthians 5:8). And we know that the Lord ascended into Heaven and has not yet returned.

Paul in the Third Heaven

So with all of these scriptural proofs, we can accurately say that when Paul was stoned in Lystra, his spirit left his body and was carried to Paradise. Paradise was in Heaven and there he heard and experienced things that could not be expressed in earthly words. Paradise contains beauty beyond words. He said he saw things and heard things that were inexpressible. One version of the Bible says they were unspeakable. The Amplified Bible says: *"He heard utterances beyond the power of man to put into words"* (2 Corinthians 12:4). He couldn't find words to explain what he saw and heard.

Paul's Hard Choice

After his visit to Paradise, I'm quite sure that Paul had a different perspective about life on earth. In fact, he told the Philippian believers very plainly that if he had a choice of whether to be in Heaven (Paradise) or to be here on earth, he would much rather be in Heaven. Then he went on to say he would stay on the earth because there was still more he needed to accomplish. He made it very clear that if he had a choice, he would rather be back in the Garden of God rather than living a life here on earth. It was only because of the call of God on his life and his desire to bring more people to Heaven that caused him to remain on earth.

> *For to me, to live is Christ, and to die is gain. But if I live on in the flesh, this will mean fruit from my labor; yet what I shall choose I cannot tell. For I am hard-pressed between the two, having a desire to depart and be with Christ, which is far better.*
>
> *Nevertheless to remain in the flesh is more needful for you. And being confident of this, I know that I shall remain and continue with you all for your progress and joy of faith.*

Philippians 1:21-25

Let me ask you this question. Why would Paul rather be in Heaven? Well, the answer is quite simple. He'd been on earth and he'd been in Heaven. By his own words, Heaven was better- so much better that in all of his letters, he could not find the words to express the beauty, the greatness, the peace, and the glory of Paradise. Paul had not even received his glorified body yet and still he would have preferred Heaven. How much more will we enjoy the presence of God and the glories of eternity when we are united with the Father, the Son, and the ones we love when we are eventually caught up like Paul into the Paradise of God.

It is interesting to note that when Paul said he was "caught up" to Paradise, he used the same Greek word *harpaz* which was used in 1 Thessalonians 4 where it says that Jesus will return and the Church will be caught up in the Rapture. I believe that Paul experienced what every believer experiences when their body ceases to function. We become absent from the body and present with the Lord in the

Garden of God in Heaven where we wait until the Father sends the Son to rapture the Church.

Paul's Thorn in the Flesh

And lest I should be exalted above measure by the abundance of the revelations, a thorn in the flesh was given to me, a messenger of Satan to buffet me, lest I be exalted above measure. Concerning this thing I pleaded with the Lord three times that it might depart from me. And He said to me, "My grace is sufficient for you, for My strength is made perfect in weakness."

2 Corinthians 12:7-9

The Apostle Paul was not only attacked by people who were trying to take his physical life, but he was also continually targeted by Satan himself who had assigned a specific demonic being to be a continual torment to Paul. Because of the abundance of the revelation that Paul received from his visit to Heaven, Satan understood what a tremendous threat Paul could be. Since Paul was armed with the revelation of God's Word and with first-hand experience of the glory of Heaven, Satan knew Paul had to be stopped. The purpose of this angelic messenger sent from Satan was to distract Paul from the calling that God had placed upon his life.

It's interesting to note that 2 Corinthians 12:7 says that the messenger of Satan was sent to "buffet" Paul. My family has been in the boating business for over a half century. I have lived almost all of my adult life near the water. Both my living room at home and my office at the church (which is several miles away) overlook a lake that has over 1,300 miles of shoreline. When a storm arises and the waves are large and white capped, the continual pounding of the waves can destroy docks and concrete sea walls. The continual pounding of the waves in a storm defines the word "buffet."

Paul experienced a continual force of repeated blows from a demonic messenger sent from Satan. Because of the pressure that Paul experienced through this continual buffeting, he asked God to make it go away, to make this attack stop. But all three times God answered Paul with the same response. God said, *"My grace is sufficient for you, for My strength is made perfect in weakness"* (2 Corinthians 12:9).

This is where God was teaching Paul that he had been given authority over all the power of the enemy. He discovered that while he was waiting for God to rebuke the enemy, as was done under the Old Covenant (Malachi 3:11), God was telling him that he, Paul, was to take authority himself and rebuke the enemy.

Paul went on to preach this principle that greater is He that is in you than he that is in the world (1 John 4:4) and that he could do all things through Christ (Philippians 4:13). We must remember that Paul the apostle didn't wake up one morning with all knowledge and understanding of the principles of the New Covenant. He himself had to be taught by the Holy Spirit and as the revelation was given to him, he wrote it down for us.

Someone may feel that if revelation brings persecution, then they would rather not have the revelation. But keep in mind that

God's power, His grace, always outperforms the enemy. Greater attacks for a Christian should not result in greater sorrow, but instead should manifest in greater victories and greater testimonies. Remember this, without a test there is no testimony. And Revelation 12:11 says they overcame him (referring to the enemy) by the blood of the Lamb and the word of their testimony.

As a Christian, we have a calling to live our life here on this earth to its fullest doing what God wants us to do and completing the mission. It is wrong for a Christian to cut their life short. However, we should live our lives knowing that we have a glorious future. We must never lose sight of the reality that Jesus has gone on before us and is preparing a place for us in His Father's kingdom where we will live a life beyond anything we can imagine. As a Christian on this earth, our best days are always ahead of us.

The Paradise of God

Chapter 11

The Promise of the Return

The age we are living in now is the Church age, the age of grace, or, as the Bible calls it, the last days (Acts 2:17). This 2,000 year time period of the last days began when Jesus ascended into Heaven and will end when Jesus returns from Heaven. Paul the apostle was living at the beginning of the last days, and we are living at the end of the last days. We are living as the generation that will experience the prophetic closure of this dispensation.

For yet a little while, and He who is coming will come and will not tarry.

Hebrews 10:37

The Last Days

The prophecies of Daniel about knowledge increasing rapidly at the end of days and the prophecies that Israel would return to its homeland have both been accomplished in a small period of time at the end of Day 6.

It is interesting to note at the time the King James Bible was printed (in the year 1611, which was in the last half of the last day), the United States did not exist, electricity did not exist, the internal combustion engine did not exist, and Israel did not exist as a nation. Up until 1611, the Bible had not been mass produced and placed in the hands of the common man. And for centuries after 1611, it had very limited distribution.

But within the last century, all of these things have come to pass. There has also been an explosion in the production of the Word of God. The Bible is the number one best-selling book in the world, and in any format it far exceeds any other publication in quantity. As the prophet Daniel predicted, we are in the middle of an explosion of knowledge and we are experiencing the "moving to and fro" he prophesied at speeds that he himself probably never imagined (Daniel 12:4).

In one generation we've moved from animal travel to space travel. We've moved from parchment to pixels. And we've moved from libraries to communication devices that are actually unlimited computers. We are definitely in the end days spoken of by the prophet Daniel.

Look at the chart, *Man's Days on the Earth* (Appendix), and you can see that Jesus was born of a virgin on earth near the end of Day 4. It's interesting to note that the physical sun was created on Day 4 and Jesus, the Son of God, was born on earth near the end of Day 4. The next two days are scripturally considered the last days, and are the days in which we are now living. The Bible also calls it the latter days because it is the last two days of man's time on the earth.

Getting Ready

Everyone who believes in Jesus Christ should be watching for the next great event to take place, and that event is the Rapture of the Church. The Rapture should not in any way be a surprise for those of us living in the last days.

> *After two days He will revive us; on the third day He will raise us up, that we may live in His sight.*
>
> *Hosea 6:2*

God's plan for the ages was established from the beginning of time. Although God had a perfect plan for man, He still had the foreknowledge of the results of man's choices and instituted a plan from the foundation of time for the redemption of mankind (Ephesians 1:3-12). The Old Testament prophets foretold the coming of the Messiah and the New Testament apostles proclaimed the return of the Messiah. We are positioned in time to experience the culmination of all of these prophecies.

Look at what Jesus said in Luke 13:32: *"Behold, I cast out demons and perform cures today and tomorrow, and the third day I shall be perfected."* Many people think that He is talking about His resurrection, and it can mean that. However, you must understand that He says today and tomorrow that He is going to perform cures, He's going to cast out demons.

Let me ask you something. Who is the body of Christ on the earth during those two days? It's us. What did Jesus say about us? He said, *"These signs will follow those who believe: In My name they will cast out demons; they will lay hands on the sick, and they will recover"* (Mark 16:17,18). Well, what is going to happen on that third day? On the third day, His kingdom is going to be perfected. The third day after the last two days is the seventh day you see on the chart. The seventh day is the one thousand year Day of the Lord where He rules and reigns on the earth perfectly.

The Day of the Lord

There are several places in the Bible that refer to the "Day of the Lord." This you have to understand: every time it says the "Day of the Lord," it's not talking about exactly the same thing. However, it is referring to something and many times it's referring to that seventh day, when He rules and reigns on this earth unrestricted in any way. This one thousand years is the Millennial reign of Christ and is called the Day of the Lord. (Because a thousand years is as a day to the Lord (2 Peter 3:8).

Where I Am, There You May Be Also

Jesus, while talking to His disciples during His last days on earth, told them He did not want them to worry or to be in stress concerning their future. He explained to them that in His Father's house in Heaven were many rooms. He went on to say that when He returned to His Father, He would prepare a place for them in His Father's house (John 14:2).

He encouraged them by telling them that He would not leave them alone or defenseless, nor would they be orphaned, but He would come back and gather them to Himself (John 14:18). He told them that wherever He would be from the time He came to get them and on throughout eternity, they would always be with Him (John 14:3).

> *Let not your heart be troubled; you believe in God, believe also in Me. In My Father's house are many mansions; if it were not so, I would have told you. I go to prepare a place for you. And if I go and prepare a place for you, I will come again and receive you to Myself; that where I am, there you may be also. And where I go you know, and the way you know.*
>
> *John 14:1-4*

In this exchange with His disciples, Jesus was laying the foundation for what the Church now calls the Rapture. A short time after Jesus told His disciples that He would return for them, He was crucified and ascended into Heaven.

The early Church taught the words of Jesus and believed that He was coming back for them. They believed and taught that He would return for those who were left behind after His ascension. However, as the Church grew and time began to pass, there were those who believed in Jesus who died. The question rose up within the Church, "If Jesus is coming back for those of us who believe in Him, what will happen to those who die before He comes back? Is there hope for them?"

Concerning Those Who Have Fallen Asleep

Paul addressed this issue when writing to the church of Thessalonica. He told them that he did not want them to be uninformed concerning Christians who died while waiting for the return of Jesus. He encouraged them by telling them that we have a hope that the world does not have (1 Thessaonians 4:13).

As believers in Jesus, we have a future and a destiny that is not available to those who reject Jesus. Paul gave the church of Thessalonica great hope by letting them know that when Jesus returns, it would make no difference whether a person had died or whether they were still alive. Either way, they would be caught up to be with the Lord forever, just as Jesus had promised His disciples in John 14.

Scoffers Will Come

Knowing this first: that scoffers will come in the last days, walking according to their own lusts, and saying, "Where is the promise of His coming? For since the fathers fell asleep, all things continue as they were from the beginning of creation."

2 Peter 3:3,4

We are in the final moments of the last days and many scoffers are speaking with loud voices. Their logic is illogical. They claim that Jesus is not coming back because He hasn't come back. They say because it has been preached in generations past that Jesus would return, and because He didn't return while they were saying

He would return, then He won't return. Their logic is flawed.

The truth is, the prophets of old and the Holy Scriptures are accurate. Jesus is coming back for His Church. While it is true that He did not come in the past when people have said He was coming, the reality is, we are closer now than ever before to His return. All of the prophecies that were to be fulfilled before His appearing have come to pass and we are now in a place where His return is imminent.

The Season of His Return

Some say that we will not know when Jesus will return because the Bible says not even the angels in Heaven know. It is true that no man knows the day or the hour of the return. No man can set a date and pinpoint a moment when Jesus will appear in the sky to gather His Church. However, the Bible clearly tells us the times and the seasons. In the same way, a farmer does not know the exact day he will harvest his crop, but he does know the season for the harvest.

We know that the season is here. Old Testament and New Testament prophecies have accurately been fulfilled and the next great event on the horizon is the appearing of the Lord in the sky, together with the saints in glory.

Don't Forget This

Peter said in verse one of chapter three of 2 Peter, "*Beloved, I now write to you this second epistle (in both of which I stir up your pure minds by way of reminder), that you may be mindful of the words which were spoken before by the holy prophets, and of the commandment of us, the apostles of the Lord and Savior."* In other words, he was saying, "I want to bring something to you by way of a reminder." A reminder is something that has been previously spoken that should have been understood and learned, but in order to make sure, a reminder is given. In this passage, Peter, who walked with Jesus, is telling us, *"Don't forget this one thing, that with the Lord one day is as a thousand years, and a thousand years as one day"* (2 Peter 3:8).

Peter is reminding us of an Old Testament principle (Ps. 90:4) and bringing it into a New Testament prophetic revelation of what was spoken by the prophet Hosea who said after two days He would raise us up, and that we would live with Him (Hosea 6:2). That parallels 1 Thessalonians 4:17 which says that once we are caught up, we will forever be with Him.

A Thief in the Night

People have been taught all their lives that no one will know when Jesus is coming back. However, let's examine what the Bible actually says in 1 Thessalonians chapter five.

> *But concerning the times and the seasons, brethren, you have no need that I should write to you.*
>
> *1 Thessalonians 5:1*

First of all, in this verse, Paul is writing to Christians. This is obvious because he refers to the reader as brethren. Then he goes on to say that there is no need he should write this, with the implication being because it is something they should already know. But like Peter in the previous passage we examined, Paul wants to make sure that these following things are understood. So even though it shouldn't be necessary for him to repeat this, he does to verify that the following statements are clearly understood.

> *For you yourselves know perfectly that the Day of the Lord so comes as a thief in the night. For when they say, "Peace and safety!" then sudden destruction comes upon them, as labor pains upon a pregnant woman. And they shall not escape.*
>
> 1 Thessalonians 5:2,3

Here, Paul is saying that the Day of the Lord will come as a thief in the night upon those who are living in peace and safety. This compares with what Jesus said comparing His return to the days of Noah (Matthew 24:37). Jesus said that in the days of Noah, people were eating and drinking, marrying and giving in marriage, and that life was going on as usual. Even though Noah had been preaching for one hundred years that the destruction of the flood was coming, his prophetic words were ignored and the people were living their lives on a day-to-day basis as usual.

Jesus was saying that the people who were ignoring the prophetic words would have sudden destruction come upon them. However, sudden destruction would not come upon Noah and his family because they believed the word of the Lord. Because they believed what God said and because they had faith in Him, when the end of days came and the flood waters were opened, they were safe in the boat and encountered no destruction.

This is the parallel given by Jesus that was reinforced by Paul when he said that as the world ignores the message of the coming of the Son of Man, living their daily lives in ignorance, then sudden destruction will come upon them and they shall not escape.

But you, brethren, are not in darkness, so that this Day should overtake you as a thief. You are all sons of light and sons of the day. We are not of the night nor of darkness.

1 Thessalonians 5:4,5

Once again, in this verse Paul is addressing Christians and telling them very clearly that this day of Christ's appearing would not overtake them as a thief in the night because they (the brethren) are sons of light and sons of the day. And because of the light and because they are watching, the appearing of the Lord will be a joyful time and not catch them off guard.

Therefore let us not sleep, as others do, but let us watch and be sober.

1 Thessalonians 5:6

Here Paul sums it up by saying that since we have the light of the Word, the prophecy of the prophets, and the understanding of what is happening, that we should be ready and watching with great anticipation for the appearing of our Lord (Romans 12:1).

Nevertheless, when the Son of Man comes, will He really find faith on the earth?

Luke 18:8

Preparing for His Return

Just because Jesus is going to return and catch you away and give you a glorified body does not give you the right, nor permission from Him, to abuse your body. Neither does it give you permission to allow your flesh to sin against the Word of God. Your body is the temple of the Holy Spirit.

> *Do you not know that your body is the temple of the Holy Spirit who is in you, whom you have from God, and you are not your own?*
>
> *1 Corinthians 6:19*

While your body is on the earth and you are waiting for Jesus to return, you must live a holy life. He desires for you to walk in faith and to present yourself physically and morally acceptable to Him, living your life as a sacrifice. Just because your body will be left behind to decay, you still have responsibility for the deeds of the flesh and for the stewardship of your physical body while you are in it.

We are told in the Scriptures that our bodies are the temple of the Holy Spirit and that we must maintain our physical body out of honor for God. If it matters to God, it should matter to us. Believing in Him and acting on His desires is faith and when Jesus returns, faith is what He will be looking for.

The Paradise of God

I beseech you therefore, brethren, by the mercies of God, that you present your bodies a living sacrifice, holy, acceptable to God, which is your reasonable service.

Romans 12:1

Reasons for Holiness

In 1 Peter 1:16, God said, *"Be holy, for I am holy."* In this passage, Christians are given the command, not a suggestion, to be holy. Holiness should never be confused with righteousness. When a person receives Jesus as their Lord and Savior, they are made righteous. Righteousness is achieved by believing (faith) in what Jesus has done for us (grace).

For by grace you have been saved through faith, and that not of yourselves; it is the gift of God.

Ephesians 2:8

While righteousness is received in a moment of time based upon what Jesus has done, holiness is achieved over a period of time, based upon our obedience to the Word of God. In other words, we could say that we are made righteous and we become holy.

It has been implied through false teaching that there is no accountability for our actions because of the grace of God. However, the Scriptures teach us otherwise. While it is true that Jesus paid the price once and for all for all sin, it's man's responsibility to turn away from sin (repent) and to live lives that are an example of the way Jesus would live. In fact, in Ephesians 5:1 we are told that we are to imitate God. In other words, if God wouldn't do it, we shouldn't do it, and if God would do it, we should do it.

To be clear, the judgment of works that a Christian goes through shortly after the Rapture is not to judge their salvation, but to judge the merit of their rewards based upon their deeds on earth.

For we must all appear before the judgment seat of Christ, that each one may receive the things done in the body, according to what he has done, whether good or bad.

2 Corinthians 5:10

As Christians, we are told that in these last days we are to be ready and watchful, looking toward the skies for the return of our Savior. But that should not be all we are doing. We should also be living a life of good works knowing that when He returns for us, there will be rewards that we either get or forfeit based upon our deeds.

And behold, I am coming quickly, and My reward is with Me, to give to every one according to his work.

Revelation 22:12

Jesus told us to let our light so shine before men that they would see our good works and glorify the Father who is in Heaven (Matthew 5:16). As we live our life of good works, a Christian can be assured that these good works will not go unnoticed, but that there will be a time of glorification through rewards in Heaven.

But you, when you pray, go into your room, and when you have shut your door, pray to your Father who is in the secret place; and your Father who sees in secret will reward you openly.

Matthew 6:6

So how does the Christian prepare for the return of Jesus? He does this in two ways. First, he must look to the skies with daily anticipation of the return (Luke 21:28). Second, he must live his life holy and acceptable, knowing that his works will not go unnoticed at the appearing of our Lord.

But the end of all things is at hand; therefore be serious and watchful in your prayers.

1 Peter 4:7

Chapter 12

The Rapture of the Church

*For our citizenship is in heaven, from which we also eagerly
wait for the Savior, the Lord Jesus Christ, who will transform
our lowly body that it may be conformed to His glorious body.*

Philippians 3:20,21

The Rapture of the Church, which is Jesus coming to catch
away the saints and take them to Heaven, is the first of
the two bookends on either side of a seven-year period.
During these seven years, the Great Tribulation is taking place on
earth and in Heaven, the giving of rewards and the Marriage Supper
of the Lamb are taking place. The second bookend on the other
side of this seven-year event is the return of Jesus with the saints
to set up His Millennial Kingdom on earth (the Second Coming).

In this chapter, we will examine the first event, the Rapture of
the Church.

*But I do not want you to be ignorant, brethren, concerning
those who have fallen asleep, lest you sorrow as others who
have no hope. For if we believe that Jesus died and rose again,
even so God will bring with Him those who sleep in Jesus.*

For this we say to you by the word of the Lord, that we who are alive and remain until the coming of the Lord will by no means precede those who are asleep.

For the Lord himself will descend from heaven with a shout, with the voice of an archangel, and with the trumpet of God. And the dead in Christ will rise first. Then we who are alive and remain shall be caught up together with them in the clouds to meet the Lord in the air. And thus we shall always be with the Lord. Therefore comfort one another with these words.

1 Thessalonians 4:13-18

Once we are caught up into the air and changed, we will be forever in resurrected bodies and together with Christ, ruling and reigning over natural mankind.

Harpazo = Rapero = Rapture

There are people who say the word "*rapture*" is not in the Bible, and because of that they say the Rapture is just fiction. While it is true that you can read the Bible from cover to cover and not find the word "*rapture*" even once, that proves absolutely nothing. The word "computer" is also not in the Bible, so does that mean computers don't exist? Of course not!

The word "*rapture*" comes from the transliteration of the Latin word *rapero* from the Vulgate Bible, a late 4th century Latin translation of the Bible. We know the languages of the Bible are Hebrew in the Old Testament and Greek in the New Testament.

The word *rapero* was translated from the original Greek word *harpazo* which means to be "caught up or snatched away." This is the word used in 1 Thessalonians 4:17.

The bottom line is this. Jesus is coming back to catch away the Church. So whether you are reading in Greek, Latin, or English it makes no difference. Jesus is coming soon to catch away the saints and take the Church to Heaven.

The Catching Away

Knowing that He who raised up the Lord Jesus will also raise us up with Jesus, and will present us with you.

2 Corinthians 4:14

Paul described to the Thessalonians how the catching away of the Church (the Rapture) will transpire. He told them that the Lord Jesus himself will descend from Heaven and that it will not be a quiet event. There would be a shout, like a shout from the voice of an archangel, and the trumpet of God will sound. When this event takes place, all of the dead bodies of everyone who believed that Jesus was the Christ will be resurrected out of the ground and caught away and ascend into the sky (1 Thessalonians 4:15-18).

Paul went on to say that the Christians who are waiting for the return of Jesus who have not yet died, will then afterwards also be caught up into the sky. When the living and dead in Christ meet Him in the air, an even more miraculous event will take place. The spirits of the saints who appear with Jesus will re-enter their bodies and the bodies of the living and dead in Christ will all be changed in a moment, in the twinkling of an eye, into resurrected bodies.

Resurrection of the Dead

So also is the resurrection of the dead. The body is sown in corruption, it is raised in incorruption. It is sown in dishonor, it is raised in glory. It is sown in weakness, it is raised in power. It is sown a natural body, it is raised a spiritual body. There is a natural body, and there is a spiritual body. And so it is written, "The first man Adam became a living being." The last Adam became a life-giving spirit.

However, the spiritual is not first, but the natural, and afterward the spiritual. The first man was of the earth, made of dust; the second Man is the Lord from heaven. As was the man of dust, so also are those who are made of dust; and as is the heavenly Man, so also are those who are heavenly. And as we have borne the image of the man of dust, we shall also bear the image of the heavenly Man.

1 Corinthians 15:42-49

The first verse of this passage is talking about the bodies of Christians who have died. When my dad passed away recently, I saw a change in his body. Angels were in the room and they escorted him to glory. His body died, but he didn't die. His spirit departed from earth and was transferred into the presence of the Lord.

The Bible talks about how Jesus was sown as a seed. His body was put in the ground into a tomb. Metaphorically it is talking about this. No matter what happens to your body, whether it goes into a casket and goes into the ground, whether it goes into a vase, or whether it gets eaten by sharks, God will raise it up on that day.

When I was a child, the concept of DNA would have been science fiction. When I was in grade school, a molecule was the smallest thing known to man. Then came the discovery of atoms, nanites, and other subatomic particles. Now there are continuing discoveries in physics that are so complex, they still aren't understood.

The body of a twelve-year-old child that lived thousands of years ago was discovered in the western United States. Although he died several thousand years ago, through samples of his DNA they discovered that he came from Asia. Mankind can take the remains of a body that has been decaying for thousands of years and tell where it came from by examining a speck of it (the DNA).

The scientific abilities of man do not even compare to the vast re-creative power contained in the words spoken by God. Regardless of what happens to your physical body, man cannot destroy and scatter something beyond God's ability to restore it. It is as though God has your DNA number and when He calls it out, your body will come back together and join with your spirit.

Sleeping in Jesus

Paul said in 1 Corinthians 15:51, *"Behold, I tell you a mystery."* This is Paul's way of getting our attention and letting us know that what he is about to say is important. *"We shall not all sleep, but we shall all be changed."* *"Sleep"* is a term in the New Testament that is used for born-again believers whose bodies have died. Spiritually they are with the Father, and though physically they are dead. The biblical term for that condition is they are "sleeping in Jesus." When Jesus comes back, the Lord will send with Him those who sleep in Jesus (1 Thessalonians 4:14).

My dad is sleeping in Jesus right now. His body is dead, but he is alive in Heaven. If Jesus were to return today, not everybody is going to be in a condition of sleeping like my dad. Some of us will still be alive. But whether you are asleep or alive, we'll all be changed.

Redemption of the Body

My spirit man has already been changed, but my body has not yet been changed.

Behold, I tell you a mystery: We shall not all sleep, but we shall all be changed—in a moment, in the twinkling of an eye, at the last trumpet. For the trumpet will sound, and the dead will be raised incorruptible, and we shall be changed. For this corruptible must put on incorruption, and this mortal must put on immortality. So when this corruptible has put on incorruption, and this mortal has put on immortality, then shall be brought to pass the saying that is written: "Death is swallowed up in victory. O Death, (the spirit of Death) where is your sting? O Hades, (the spirit of Hades) where is your victory?

1 Corinthians 15:51-55

In other words, Death has not been swallowed up in victory yet, because we haven't had the complete redemption. Our spirits have been redeemed, because Christ has redeemed us from the curse of the law (Galatians 3:13). The Bible also says that we are eagerly awaiting the adoption and redemption of the body (Romans 8:23). We are currently between redemptions. The redemption of our spirit is in our past and the redemption of our body is in our future. When that last redemption takes place at the Rapture, Death will be swallowed up and then our redemption will be complete. For the Church, Death's sting no longer has power because Death is swallowed up in victory!

> *Now may the God of peace Himself sanctify you completely; and may your whole spirit, soul, and body be preserved blameless at the coming of our Lord Jesus Christ. He who calls you is faithful, who also will do it.*
>
> *1 Thessalonians 5:23,24*

Coming on the Clouds

When Jesus appears in the sky, the Scriptures tell us that we will be caught up to meet Him in the clouds. That's not talking about precipitation, moisture, or weather conditions, but rather clouds of glory. Also, it is interesting that the word "cloud" is used in the New Testament to identify the spirits of those waiting in Heaven for their glorified bodies. The Bible says we are surrounded by a cloud of witnesses.

Therefore we also, since we are surrounded by so great a cloud of witnesses, let us lay aside every weight, and the sin which so easily ensnares us, and let us run with endurance the race that is set before us.

Hebrews 12:1

Over the years I have officiated countless funerals of Christians. Many times after the service we follow the hearse to the cemetery where the casket that contains the body of the one who had died is placed in the ground. While their body was placed in the ground and is waiting for the resurrection, the spirit of the deceased is in Heaven with the Lord and is a part of the cloud of witnesses that is still thinking, talking, understanding, looking on, and cheering us on.

Transformed into New Bodies

So, Jesus will appear in the sky with the spirits of all of the Christians who have passed on. Their bodies are somewhere on the earth – in a box, an urn, or even in the sea. Because of natural disasters and war, some bodies have never been recovered; however, their DNA particles are on earth somewhere. God will resurrect their bodies, wherever their remains are, and they will be gathered back together in the form of a body and their body will be caught up into the air, glorified and reunited with their spirit.

So the dead in Christ will rise first. Then we who are alive and remain (the believers) shall be caught up together with them in the clouds to meet the Lord in the air.

1 Thessalonians 4:16,17, emphasis mine

I think it is very interesting in this account of the Church being caught up into the sky that we are told that the resurrection of the dead will take place first. Then later, there will be the catching away of those who are alive and the two groups together in the air will receive their glorified bodies. Although these two events are connected, Paul was very specific in telling us that they would not happen at exactly the same time. The dead in Christ will be resurrected first, then the remaining Christians who are still living will be caught up.

Why would we need to know this? I believe the answer is quite simple and somewhat practical. I think the reason the Word tells us that the dead in Christ will rise first is so those of us who are still alive and remain will not be alarmed or fearful when we see it happen. We have some prophetic warning, so to speak.

In the Twinkling of an Eye

Whether a believer has already died, or whether a believer is still alive at the return of Jesus, we will all be changed. It says, *"in a moment, in the twinkling of an eye"* (1 Corinthians 15:52). I don't believe that scripture is talking about the rate of speed at which we are going to be caught up, but it is talking about the rate of speed we are going to be changed. It says in that moment, corruption drops off and we take on incorruption. Mortality drops off and we take on immortality (1 Corinthians 15:53). In that moment we become as He is!

Most Christian movies that have been made about the Rapture have everyone shooting up into the air in a split second, like out of a catapult, but that's not how the Bible says it is going to happen. When Jesus ascended into Heaven, He had been talking to His disciples. As they stood there watching Him, He was taken up into the clouds in the sky (Acts 1:9-11). It says as He was saying these things, He began to ascend and then He was gone. They watched Him go. What did the two angels say who were standing by? They said, *"In the same way He left, He is coming back."* (vs. 11). I believe Jesus is our example in many ways. The body He has is the kind of body we're going to have. But in the same way He ascended, I believe is the way we are going to ascend.

Glorified to Be Like Jesus

These resurrected bodies will be like the glorified body that Jesus Christ, the Son of God, obtained when He put His blood on the mercy seat in Heaven on the day of His resurrection (Hebrews 9:12). We (the Church) will be like Him for all eternity! Because the Bible says we will be like Him, we now have great insight into what our new glorified, resurrected bodies will be like. Simply put, we will be like Jesus (1 John 3:2).

So, what was the resurrected body of Jesus like? We have scriptural verification about this because after Jesus received His glorified body, He spent forty days with His disciples on earth before ascending into Heaven (Acts 1:3).

His glorified, resurrected body was not restricted by the laws of earthly physics. He could appear at the speed of thought; He could move through solid walls (John 20:19); gravity had no power over Him (Acts 1:9); He ate fish (John 21:13-15), while at the same time His body had substance (Luke 24:39).

At one point, He told His disciples to handle Him and feel Him and understand that His body was flesh and bone (Luke 24:39). He did not say flesh and blood as would be the normal statement. That was because His blood had already been placed on the altar in Heaven (Hebrews 9:12) making Him the once-and-for-all sacrifice for all mankind. He paid the debt we could not pay with the perfect blood that we did not have.

> *But Christ came as High Priest of the good things to come, with the greater and more perfect tabernacle not made with hands, that is, not of this creation. Not with the blood of goats and calves, but with His own blood He entered the Most Holy Place once for all, having obtained eternal redemption.*
>
> *Hebrews 9:11,12*

Moving On to Heaven

The Rapture happens at the beginning of the seven-year period. Then what happens? We go back to Heaven. We now have our resurrected bodies like Jesus has and just like Jesus ascended, we go into Heaven for seven years. While we're in Heaven for seven years, there are still people here on the earth because not everybody got raptured. Only those who believe in Jesus Christ as their Messiah will go in the Rapture. Everyone who trusts Jesus as their Savior will be caught up in the Rapture because no believer will be left behind.

> *For God did not appoint us to wrath, but to obtain salvation through our Lord Jesus Christ, who died for us, that whether we wake or sleep, we should live together with Him.*

> *1 Thessalonians 5:9,10*

When the Rapture occurs, the Church age is over. We are the glorified body people; we become like super-heroes. We are super-human. We are as He is. We have a body like Jesus and we're in Heaven with the Lord.

Trophies of His Grace

> *So God can point to us in all future ages as examples of the incredible wealth of His grace and kindness toward us, as shown in all He has done for us who are united with Christ Jesus.*

> *Ephesians 2:7 (NLT)*

In the ages to come, God will display His Church as a manifestation and trophy of His grace toward man. The Church will forever be an example of the goodness of God and of the perfection of the promise of His Word. The Church, His Body, His Bride will give Him glory throughout all of the ages.

Jesus is not a polygamist. He has one Bride, and that Bride is the Church.

And now that He has snatched away His Bride, He will take her to His Father's house where He will complete His promise to her. She will accept the gift and they will be one for all eternity (John 17:22-23).

The Church Is Unique

The entity of the Church is like no other group throughout all of history. God's plan and design for people to receive salvation based on His grace instead of works or sacrifices, to be joint heirs with Him, to rule and reign with Him out of the New Jerusalem in glorified, resurrected, supernatural bodies is almost beyond comprehension. Yet, until the Church is raptured, that opportunity is still open.

The Bible tells us that after the Rapture of the Church, the world will experience the greatest harvest of souls ever known (Revelation 7:9-10). No doubt, once people see that the gospel they had heard about is actually true and that the catching away of the Church really happened, they will decide to be on the side of Christ. However, they won't be a part of the Church. They will live on earth, but will not have the supernatural bodies and abilities of those who were born again before the Rapture, nor will they escape the wrath that is coming. Don't bypass this amazing opportunity.

The Paradise of God

Chapter 13

The Seven Years in Heaven

Your dead shall live; together with my dead body they shall arise. Awake and sing, you who dwell in dust; for your dew is like the dew of herbs, and the earth shall cast out the dead.

Come, my people, enter your chambers, and shut your doors behind you; hide yourself, as it were, for a little moment, until the indignation is past. For behold, the Lord comes out of His place to punish the inhabitants of the earth for their iniquity; the earth will also disclose her blood, and will no more cover her slain.

Isaiah 26:19-21

There is a small sliver of time between the last days and the Millennial reign of Christ consisting of seven years. At the beginning of this seven-year period, Jesus appears in the sky and catches up the Church to be with Him (the Rapture). At the end of the seven-year period, Jesus returns to the earth with the Church and touches down in Jerusalem on the Mount of Olives (the Second Coming).

During this seven-year time period, three major things take

place. The first two events take place in Heaven. They are the Judgment Seat of Christ and the Marriage Supper of the Lamb. The third event takes place on the earth during this seven years and is a time of great turmoil led by the Antichrist. It is called the Great Tribulation (Matthew 24:21). The Church is not involved in any way with the Tribulation until the last day of the seven years when Jesus returns to the earth with the Church. While with Jesus for this seven-year period, the Church will be excluded from wrath on earth, but experience great comfort and joy in Heaven (1 Thessalonians 5:9).

After the Rapture of the Church, the destiny and location of all born-again Christians is easy to follow. Why? Because the Bible tells us in 1 Thessalonians 4:17 that when the Church is caught up to meet the Lord in the air, from that point on we will always be with Him.

> *Then we who are alive and remain shall be caught up together with them in the clouds to meet the Lord in the air. And thus we shall always be with the Lord.*

> *1 Thessalonians 4:17*

From the Rapture of the Church until eternity, the Church, His body, His Bride, is with Him. If you are a Christian and you want to know where you will be throughout the remainder of recorded history and into eternity, as you read about future events in the Bible, wherever Christ is, you will be in close proximity.

Heavenly Jerusalem

The first two events in the seven-year period take place in Heaven or more specifically, the Heavenly Jerusalem. The Heavenly Jerusalem is not to be confused with the New Jerusalem that comes down from God out of Heaven after the Millennium. During the Great Tribulation, the temple of God is opened in Heaven and the original Ark of the Covenant is seen in the temple in the Heavenly Jerusalem (Revelation 11:19). This lets us know that this is not the New Jerusalem because the New Jerusalem does not have a temple (Revelation 21:22-23).

This scripture is referring to the Heavenly Jerusalem:

Then the temple of God was opened in heaven, and the ark of His covenant was seen in His temple. And there were lightnings, noises, thunderings, an earthquake, and great hail.

Revelation 11:19

This scripture is referring to the New Jerusalem:

But I saw no temple in it, for the Lord God Almighty and the Lamb are its temple. The city had no need of the sun or of the moon to shine in it, for the glory of God illuminated it. The Lamb is its light.

Revelation 21:22,23

The First Event in Heaven:
The Judgment Seat of Christ

In Paul's letter to the Christians at the church of Corinth, he clearly told them that there would be a time when they would stand before the Lord Jesus in judgment, and would be judged by their actions, whether they were good or bad.

> *Therefore we make it our aim, whether present or absent, to be well pleasing to Him. For we must all appear before the judgment seat of Christ, that each one may receive the things done in the body, according to what he has done, whether good or bad.*
>
> *2 Corinthians 5:9,10*

Recently, while speaking at a conference, a man came to me at the end of a meeting and informed me that he would not be judged. He continued by explaining why. He said, "I have already been judged. I have been cleansed of my sins, and I will not be at the Great White Throne Judgment." He was a little surprised when I said I completely agreed with him.

Because he had accepted Jesus as his Lord and Savior, old things had passed away and all things had become new. He was cleansed of all sin and his salvation would never have to be judged. He was right that he will not be at the Great White Throne Judgment because that judgment takes place at the end of the thousand year reign of Christ on earth, after the resurrection of the unrighteous dead. That judgment is for all of the unrighteous dead throughout history and for the people born in the Millennium who have not gone through any prior judgment.

The Great White Throne Judgment is not what Paul was talking about in his letter to the Corinthians. Paul was simply saying that even though our eternal salvation is secure because of the work of Jesus, we as Christians will still be held accountable for the deeds of our flesh. Although the Judgment Seat of Christ is not where our salvation is judged, it is where our works are judged and that will determine the rewards that we receive.

> *But why do you judge your brother? Or why do you show contempt for your brother? For we shall all stand before the judgment seat of Christ.*
>
> *Romans 14:10*

In Revelation, Jesus said that He is coming quickly and that He is bringing with Him rewards that He will give to each person individually according to what they have done (Revelation 22:12). Who is He coming back for? According to 1 Thessalonians chapter four, He will descend from Heaven and gather together His body (the Church). The reward He is bringing with Him is not salvation, because the Church already has that, and salvation is based upon what He did on the cross. By His own words, rewards are something different based upon what we have done while on the earth.

> *For the Son of Man will come in the glory of His Father with His angels, and then He will reward each according to his works.*
>
> *Matthew 16:27*

185

As we stand before the Lord giving an account for our deeds, the age-old excuses we use on earth will be worthless. We can give Him the reasons why we did or didn't do what He asked, but there will be no excuse. Remember, Jesus said the rewards that He is bringing with Him will be distributed to each individual according to what he has done, not according to what he has intended to do.

As a born-again believer, you should rejoice when you see the Lord appear in the air knowing that you will forever be with Him. But there will be a greater joy in knowing that you have pleased Him by doing what He asked. Remember, Jesus is the one who asked His disciples, "*Why do you call Me Lord and not do what I ask you to do?*" (Luke 6:46). Our obedience is important to Him.

Cleansed but Accountable

I am a strong believer in grace. Without grace, there is no hope for us. Grace is the power of God that allows us to accomplish the impossible. But grace cannot be the defense we use when we stand at the Judgment Seat of Christ and give an account of our actions. Because of His grace, we who are Christians are absolved from all punishment of sin and should not have sin-consciousness in our daily lives. But just because we have been cleansed of all sin does not excuse us from accountability for our actions.

Although it may seem like a paradox that we have been cleansed but are still accountable, we cannot ignore the truth that faith pleases God (Hebrews 11:6) and faith without works is dead (James 2:17). While there will be no future judgment for sin for a Christian, there will be rewards for obedience.

186

But without faith it is impossible to please Him, for he who comes to God must believe that He is, and that He is a rewarder of those who diligently seek Him.

Hebrews 11:6

Rewards

Remember this. A reward is a good thing. There was a story reported in the media of a young man who found a briefcase with a name on it. Without opening it and looking inside, he walked several blocks in a crowded city and took it to the man whose name and address was on a tag on the outside. Little did the young man know that the briefcase contained over $500,000 in stocks and securities. He was given a $5,000 reward.

The young man evidently had been raised in a home where he was trained by word and example concerning character and integrity. He tried to refuse the reward, but the businessman was so thankful because of the righteousness of the young man that he insisted that he take it.

When the Father looks at a born-again believer, He sees the righteousness of Christ within him. He seeks to give the same honor as He would give His own Son. In fact, the Bible says that for those of us who believe, we are joint heirs with Christ (Romans 8:17).

Much in the same way, Jesus Christ seeks to honor, by way of a reward, all of those who have been obedient to the work that

He has given them. Every gift from Heaven is good and perfect (James 1:17).

> *When the Chief Shepherd appears, you will receive the crown of glory that does not fade away.*
>
> *1 Peter 5:4*

Rewards at the Judgment Seat of Christ

God is generous and throughout His Word, He has always blessed and rewarded those who have been obedient to His commands. He told Abram in a vision that he should not fear because He would protect him, and that He himself would be an exceedingly great reward to Abram.

In Proverbs 13:13, we are told that a man who despises the Word will be destroyed, but that the one who fears the commandment of God will be rewarded. In Proverbs 25:22, we are told that there is a reward from the Lord for those who walk in kindness toward their enemies. Jesus said that we are to love our enemies and to do good and that we are to be lenders and in doing so, we will receive a great reward.

> *Finally, there is laid up for me the crown of righteousness, which the Lord, the righteous Judge, will give to me on that Day, and not to me only but also to all who have loved His appearing.*
>
> *2 Timothy 4:8*

There are many scriptures that talk about the rewards that a

Christian will receive in Heaven at the Judgment Seat of Christ. The Scriptures talk about great rewards, full rewards, and just rewards. But one thing is for sure, any reward that Jesus has for the believer will be magnificently perfect and personally designed for the one receiving it. It will be desirable and everything that can be done in this life to obtain such a reward should be done.

Simply stated, walking in true holiness and obedience to God's Word will bring a reward at the Judgment Seat of Christ and walking in disobedience to God's Word will eliminate the possibility of receiving God's perfect gift.

Let no one cheat you of your reward, taking delight in false humility and worship of angels, intruding into those things which he has not seen, vainly puffed up by his fleshly mind.

Colossians 2:18

It is important for Christians to understand clearly that there will be accountability for their actions. While our salvation is based clearly on the work of Jesus, our rewards are a result of our actions. And while many have been taught the security of their salvation, there has been an assumption of entitlement concerning eternal gifts from God.

As Christians in these last days, we must be an example of the goodness of God and He will be glorified through our actions. Let no one deceive you. Your good works will be noticed, remembered, and placed in a ledger in your account in Heaven and in due time, you will receive your reward.

The following is a list of scriptures that should encourage you to do good works.

Heavenly Rewards

Blessed are you when they revile and persecute you, and say all kinds of evil against you falsely for My sake. Rejoice and be exceedingly glad, for great is your reward in heaven, for so they persecuted the prophets who were before you.

Matthew 5:11,12

But love your enemies, do good, and lend, hoping for nothing in return; and your reward will be great, and you will be sons of the Most High. For He is kind to the unthankful and evil.

Luke 6:35

"Refrain your voice from weeping, and your eyes from tears; for your work shall be rewarded," says the LORD.

Jeremiah 31:16

Blessed are you when men hate you, and when they exclude you, and revile you, and cast out your name as evil, for the Son of Man's sake. Rejoice in that day and leap for joy! For indeed your reward is great in heaven, for in like manner their fathers did to the prophets.

Luke 6:22,23

For if I preach the gospel, I have nothing to boast of, for necessity is laid upon me; yes, woe is me if I do not preach the gospel! For if I do this willingly, I have a reward; but if against my will, I have been entrusted with a stewardship.

1 Corinthians 9:17

But you, when you pray, go into your room, and when you have shut your door, pray to your Father who is in the secret place; and your Father who sees in secret will reward you openly.

Matthew 6:6

(By faith Moses) esteeming the reproach of Christ greater riches than the treasures in Egypt; for he looked to the reward.

Hebrews 11:26

He who receives a prophet in the name of a prophet shall receive a prophet's reward. And he who receives a righteous man in the name of a righteous man shall receive a righteous man's reward.

Matthew 10:41

Now he who plants and he who waters are one, and each one will receive his own reward according to his own labor.1 Corinthians 3:8Then I said, "I have labored in vain, I have spent my strength for nothing and in vain; Yet surely my just reward is with the Lord, and my work with my God."

Isaiah 49:4

The evil man gets rich for the moment, but the good man's reward lasts forever.

Proverbs 11:18 (TLB)

Therefore do not cast away your confidence, which has great reward.

Hebrews 10:35

Holiness vs. Righteousness

The rewards are only for the righteous. Only those who have been made righteous will be at the Judgment Seat of Christ and be qualified to receive a reward. The rewards will be based on holiness.

Remember, for the Christian, righteousness is a gift from God that they receive at salvation and it is based upon the work of the cleansing blood of Jesus. Righteousness does not increase, but is a condition that is established at the new birth and is received in its fullness.

For He made Him who knew no sin to be sin for us, that we might become the righteousness of God in Him.

2 Corinthians 5:21

Holiness, on the other hand, is a choice and a Christian should grow in holiness day by day. Holiness is achieved by being obedient to the Word of God and by living a life of submission to God's desires and commands. As a Christian grows in faith through the hearing of God's Word, holiness increases. Our eternal rewards are based on our holiness.

Good Works

So when you hear that still small voice from within telling you to forgive, to repent, to be obedient, or to do something specific, don't ignore the voice of the Holy Spirit. Your rewards depend upon your obedience to His Word.

> *Each one's work will become clear; for the Day will declare it, because it will be revealed by fire; and the fire will test each one's work, of what sort it is. If anyone's work which he has built on it endures, he will receive a reward.*
>
> *1 Corinthians 3:13,14*

The good work you do here on earth will endure. For example, I remember a Sunday long ago (before I was a pastor) when I was looking forward to coming to church to hear the sermon that day. But as I entered the front doors, I was met by the Children's Church coordinator, who said, "We're short a teacher in the junior high Sunday School class. Would you be able to teach in there today?" Inside I was feeling, *You have to be kidding me! I don't want to teach; I want to hear a good sermon!* But instead of responding with that selfish attitude, I decided to teach the children with the best I had to give them.

Someone might think that nobody really remembers service like that. They may be right that nobody remembers it – except God. But that is a work that will endure. Don't ever think that what you do for the Lord is not remembered. If the work is good, it endures and you will receive a reward.

However, if the same work is done with a bad attitude and not as a service to the Lord, it might not qualify for a reward. *"If anyone's work is burned* (it doesn't measure up), *he will suffer loss* (loss of the reward)*; but he himself will be saved, yet so as through fire* (by the skin of his teeth) (1 Corinthians 3:15) (emphasis mine).

You must continue to do good works. Even if it looks like no one appreciates it, God appreciates it and He will not forget what you "do heartily as to the Lord" and there will be a reward for you. Once again, the reward we are referring to is not your salvation.

> *And whatever you do, do it heartily, as to the Lord and not to men, knowing that from the Lord you will receive the reward of the inheritance; for you serve the Lord Christ. But he who does wrong will be repaid for what he has done, and there is no partiality.*
>
> *Colossians 3:23–25*

The Next Event in Heaven
The Marriage Supper of the Lamb

The Judgment Seat of Christ is a part of the preparation of the Bride for the marriage to the Bridegroom. The rewards are a part of the adornment. The Church is the Bride of Christ. The time for the marriage of the Lamb has come. His wife has made herself ready (Revelation 19:7).

The Bride of Christ

Husbands, love your wives, just as Christ also loved the church and gave himself for her, that He might sanctify and cleanse her with the washing of water by the word, that He might present her to himself a glorious church, not having spot or wrinkle or any such thing, but that she should be holy and without blemish.

Ephesians 5:25-27

This verse in Ephesians tells us several things about the relationship between Christ and the Church. First of all, it parallels that husbands should love their wives in the same way that Christ loved the Church. Jesus said that the greatest love a person could demonstrate would be to lay down their life for someone else (John 15:13). And that is what Jesus did for the Church. He did that so that she would be cleansed, and so that He could present her (the Church) to himself, pure and spotless.

The Church is obviously the love of Jesus' life. He prayed to His Father that He could be one with those who believed in Him. The believers are the Church. He prophesied that He was going to His Father's house to prepare a place for her, which is exactly what a young Jewish man would do for his love. In the same way a young Jewish man would snatch away his bride, Jesus said He was coming back for those who believed in Him and He would take them to His Father's house. The Church is obviously His Bride.

Before Jesus returns to earth with the saints to set up His

195

Millennial Kingdom, the Apostle John was shown by revelation an event that was to take place in Heaven.

> *"Let us be glad and rejoice and give Him glory, for the marriage of the Lamb has come, and His wife has made herself ready." And to her it was granted to be arrayed in fine linen, clean and bright, for the fine linen is the righteous acts of the saints. Then he said to me, "Write: 'Blessed are those who are called to the marriage supper of the Lamb!'" And he said to me, "These are the true sayings of God."*
>
> *Revelation 19:7-9*

Jewish Wedding Customs

The concept of the Marriage Supper of the Lamb becomes more understandable when we view it in terms of the Jewish wedding customs in the days of Jesus. Generally, the wedding had three major parts. First, a dowry would be paid to the bride or her family and a contract was agreed upon by the parents of the bride and the bridegroom. This action began the time of betrothal. Today in western culture, it would correspond to the time of engagement. It was during this time of betrothal between Joseph and Mary that she was found to be with Child (Luke 2:5).

The second part of the Jewish custom in marriage occurred a year later. At this time, the bridegroom and his male friends would go to the house of the bride during the night. The bride would know that he was coming and was to be ready, but she did not know the exact time of his arrival. In order for her to be taken to the bridegroom's house, she had to be ready when the bridegroom arrived. When he arrived, the bride and her party would follow the bridegroom and his men to the bridegroom's house.

The last phase is the marriage supper itself. The marriage supper and the celebration that followed usually lasted for seven days. Many people were invited to this time of celebration, but only the ones who accepted the invitation to the father's house were a part of the wedding celebration.

In the same way, when we receive Jesus as our Lord and Savior, it is a type of betrothal and we are to be ready, waiting, and looking forward to our "abduction" (rapture) by the Bridegroom. He will take us to His Father's house where He has prepared a place for us (John 14:1-4). For one week (Daniel's 70th week), we will celebrate our union with Him in Heaven.

The Bride of Christ

Husbands, love your wives, just as Christ also loved the Church and gave himself for her (Ephesians 5:25).

A Jewish Bride	The Church, the Bride of Christ
Dowry paid by the bridegroom	Jesus paid the price in full for His Bride
Contract signed between the two parties	Salvation: Contract signed Jesus signed with His blood We sign with our faith
Betrothal Period (the time of waiting for the bridegroom after the contract is signed)	Time of waiting (after salvation) for the Rapture
Bridegroom comes to get the bride at her house	Jesus comes to get the Church on earth (Rapture)
Bridegroom takes the bride to his father's house	Jesus (Bridegroom) takes the Church (His Bride) to Heaven (His Father's house)
Marriage supper and celebration for seven days	Marriage Supper of the Lamb Daniel's 70th week (7 years in Heaven)

When you receive Jesus as your Lord and Savior, it is like becoming betrothed to Him. While we wait for His arrival, living out our lives on earth, He will appear at "our house" and take us to His Father's house where the prayer of the Bridegroom in John 17 will be fulfilled. The Church will be united with Jesus and there will be a major celebration in Heaven.

Father, I desire that they also whom You gave Me may be with Me where I am, that they may behold My glory which You have given Me; for You loved Me before the foundation of the world.

John 17:2

The Invitation

Then he said to me, "Write: 'Blessed are those who are called to the marriage supper of the Lamb!'"

Revelation 19:9

Attending the wedding feast will ,of course, be the King of kings (the Lamb) and His glorious Bride (the Church), but there will also be others invited. They include the spirits of the Old Testament saints, the spirits of the martyred dead of the Tribulation, whose bodies are going to be raised at the Second Coming, and of course the angels and the heavenly hosts. The Marriage Supper of the Lamb will be a glorious and blessed celebration.

Preparation of the Church in Heaven

While in Heaven for seven years, there will be activity as the Church is taught and trained for the return to earth with the Lord. All of the information needed to reign and rule will not be automatically downloaded like a computer update. Schooling will be necessary.

When you became a Christian, the Spirit of the Lord moved into your spirit to live forever. However, just because you were born again, you did not automatically have all the knowledge of God. What you did have was the Holy Spirit living in you as the Revealer of the Word that you read and hear. Revelation is not automatic, study is required; however, because of the Spirit within, truth and understanding is obtained. When our bodies are glorified (born again) the same principle will apply. We will continue to learn about the things of God for all eternity.

While everything the Church is experiencing in Heaven is glorious during this seven-year period, on earth great devastation is taking place and life is difficult for everyone there.

Chapter 14

The Seven Years on the Earth
The Great Tribulation

Beginning with the Rapture of the Church and ending with the Second Coming of Jesus is a seven-year period on earth referred to as the Great Tribulation. During this same seven-year period, the Church will be in Heaven enjoying the Marriage Supper of the Lamb, hidden away until the indignation and devastation has passed.

These seven years are divided into two periods of three and one-half years each (1260 days or 42 months). The greatest devastation during the Tribulation will take place during the last three and one-half years, when the Antichrist will do his best to rule on the earth and to place his throne in the temple of God.

The Ultimate Desire of the Antichrist

The Antichrist still has one prize that he wants and that is Jerusalem, the apple of God's eye. On the holy mountain is the spot where the Ark of the Covenant sat and on that same location was the threshing floor of David. Many ancient Jewish sages believe that it was also the location where Adam was created, the location where Abraham went to sacrifice Isaac, and the location of Jacob's ladder to Heaven.[2]

In the temple was a place called the holy of holies. It was a place that only the high priest entered once a year. It contained the Ark of the Covenant and the glory of God was manifest in this room. After the future rebuilding of the temple, the Antichrist will attempt to place his throne in this holy place. But just like in Isaiah chapter 14 when Lucifer attempted to place his throne on the sides of the north on the holy mountain of God and was cast out of Heaven, likewise will ultimately fail in Jerusalem.

The religion of Islam has attempted to make the world believe that Jerusalem is a holy place to them. However, the city of Jerusalem is not mentioned once in the Koran. When Muslims pray, they face Mecca and not Jerusalem. Islam was never mentioned in the Bible because the religion of Islam did not even exist until over half a millennium (five hundred years) after Jesus was on the earth. Jerusalem is God's holy city that He gave to His chosen people, the children of Israel.

The Spirit of Grace on Jerusalem

Although the age of grace (the Church age) ends at the Rapture, the Spirit of grace never ends. And this is shown by God's relentless pursuit of His chosen people.

---

[2]Israel Ariel and Chaim Richman, *Carta's Illustrated Encyclopedia of the Holy Temple in Jerusalem*, (Israel: The Temple Institute and Carta, Jerusalem, 2005), pages 2, 5, 6, 18.

Many Bible scholars believe the Battle of Ezekiel 38 will usher in the beginning of the Great Tribulation. This seven-year period, also known as Daniel's 70th week and "a week of years," will take place immediately preceding the Second Coming. During the first 42 months of the seven-year Tribulation, the Jews will build a temple and resume the sacrifice of animals in an attempt to correctly obey the law.

And he shall enter into a strong and firm covenant with the many for one week [seven years]. And in the midst of the week he shall cause the sacrifice and offering to cease [for the remaining three and one-half years]; and upon the wing or pinnacle of abominations [shall come] one who makes desolate, until the full determined end is poured out on the desolator.

Daniel 9:27 (AMP)

According to Daniel 9:27, the Antichrist will cause the sacrifices to cease in the middle of the week (the Tribulation). Near the end of the second forty-two month section of the Great Tribulation (the end of the week), the Lord will open the eyes of His chosen people (the Jews) and they will receive the Lord as Messiah in preparation for His return. Because of His love and His promise, He will pour out the Spirit of grace on Jerusalem.

And I will pour on the house of David and on the inhabitants of Jerusalem the Spirit of grace and supplication; then they will look on Me whom they pierced. Yes, they will mourn for

Him as one mourns for his only son, and grieve for Him as one grieves for a firstborn.

Zechariah 12:10

What Is the Purpose of the Tribulation?

The focus of the Great Tribulation is primarily three-fold. It is for the judgment of the Gentiles, for the evangelism of the world, and for the conversion of Israel.

The Old Testament prophets referred to it as the time of Jacob's trouble (Jeremiah 30:7), but Jesus coined the phrase Great Tribulation in Matthew 24:21. Jesus said it would be a time of unparalleled turmoil and destruction on the earth, but in the end, Israel will be saved.

"In all history there has never been such a time of terror. It will be a time of trouble for my people Israel. Yet in the end they will be saved! For in that day," says the Lord of Heaven's Armies, "I will break the yoke from their necks and snap their chains. Foreigners will no longer be their masters. For my people will serve the Lord their God and their king descended from David—the king I will raise up for them.""

Jeremiah 30:7-9 (NLT)

"For I am with you and will save you," says the LORD. "I will completely destroy the nations where I have scattered you, but I

will not completely destroy you. I will discipline you, but with justice; I cannot let you go unpunished."

Jeremiah 30:11

Paul said in his writings to the church in Thessalonica that likewise the church would be avenged during the tribulation for the persecution that they had endured.

It is a righteous thing with God to repay with tribulation those who trouble you, and to give you who are troubled rest with us when the Lord Jesus is revealed from heaven with His mighty angels, in flaming fire taking vengeance on those who do not know God, and on those who do not obey the gospel of our Lord Jesus Christ.

These shall be punished with everlasting destruction from the presence of the Lord and from the glory of His power, when He comes, in that Day, to be glorified in His saints and to be admired among all those who believe, because our testimony among you was believed.

2 Thessalonians 1:6-10

While many people think the Tribulation will involve the Church, the Bible does not provide support for this theory. Instead, the Bible teaches at least a three-fold purpose for the Great Tribulation and none of them involve the Church. The New Testament teaches that the Church will be taken at the Rapture to be with the Lord before the Tribulation begins, because God has not destined the Church for wrath. While other groups of redeemed people will go through the Tribulation, the Church, the Bride of Christ, will not.

> *Much more then, having now been justified by His blood, we shall be saved from wrath through Him.*

Romans 5:9

> *To wait for His Son from heaven, whom He raised from the dead, even Jesus who delivers us from the wrath to come.*

1 Thessalonians 1:10

> *Because you have kept My command to persevere, I also will keep you from the hour of trial which shall come upon the whole world, to test those who dwell on the earth.*

Revelation 3:10

While the Antichrist is attempting to deceive the world and prevent the promise of God from being fulfilled, great evangelism is also taking place on the earth. There will be 12,000 Jewish men from each of the twelve tribes (144,000) who, along with angels and the two witnesses, will proclaim the truth of the Messiah to the entire world. This will produce a great harvest of souls, to numerous to count – from every tribe, nation, tongue, and people – all from the tribulation (Revelation 7:9-17). Jesus said, *"This gospel of the kingdom will be preached in all the world as a witness to all the nations, and then the end* (Second Coming) *will come"* (Matt. 24:14).

Annihilation of the Enemy

You must understand that the Antichrist never completely accomplishes what he sets out to do. Near the end of the Tribulation, there is great confusion in his camp. He has not been successful in taking over the earth (Revelation 6:8). He has been dealing with the 144,000 Jewish evangelists, the two witnesses, and angels preaching the gospel (Revelation 7:4; Revelation 11:3-6; Revelation 14:6). Also he has had rebellion in his inner circle, but he has not given up. While he is struggling to conquer the holy place of God, his end is drawing near. Like lightning from the east that flashes to the west, the Son of Man, along with His angels and His Church, descends from Heaven to the Mount of Olives and annihilates the enemy, marking the end of the Tribulation on earth (Revelation 20:9,10).

The Book of Revelation

John the apostle was a close friend of Jesus. They spent years together and because John was in the inner circle of the ministry of Jesus, he no doubt had many personal discussions that were not recorded in the gospels. Several decades after Jesus ascended into Heaven, John received a vision from God while exiled on Patmos, an island in the Aegean Sea. This revelation became known as the Book of Revelation or the Apocalypse. It is the final book in the Bible.

Throughout history there has been a wrong perception of the book of Revelation. It has been portrayed in novels and theater as a revelation of evil and a time when fear rules and reigns over the

Church. Many have focused on Satan, 666, devastation, and the Antichrist and what he does on the earth. This has incorrectly instilled fear into the hearts of many people. As a result, many Christians have ignored reading and studying the book of Revelation, relinquishing it to a place of obscurity.

The truth is, the book of Revelation is not a book about the evils of the Antichrist, but instead is a book of the victory of Jesus Christ. It is the revelation of Jesus Christ, not the revelation of the Antichrist. It is interesting that the word "antichrist" does not appear once in the Book of Revelation.

John said that anyone who reads and hears the words of the prophecy contained in this book will be blessed (Revelation 1:3). There is a blessing that comes from reading and meditating on God's Word concerning the end times. The book of Revelation is a book of victory and many Christians miss blessings in life because they fail to read it.

I would like to encourage everyone who is reading this book to also read the book of Revelation. It begins with Jesus appearing in the sky and taking His Church into Heaven. Much of the book of Revelation tells of the trials and failures of the Antichrist as he attempts to conquer the holy city of Jerusalem.

The good news is while all this tribulation is taking place on earth, the Church is basking in the glory of God and experiencing the joys of Heaven, while preparing for the kingdom of God to be manifest on earth. I've had people accuse me of believing in escape theology. They have said that I teach that one of the benefits of being a Christian is that we are caught up to Heaven and escape the Tribulation. My response is this: guilty as charged! Actually, that's one of the benefits of becoming a Christian. We receive everlasting life and joy and escape the Tribulation and death. But we don't just survive, we overcome! As overcomers, we reign with Him in the Millennial Kingdom for a thousand years.

The book of Revelation ends with the defeat of Satan, the elimination of death, and the ushering in of eternity. There is a new Heaven and a new earth and the New Jerusalem (Revelation 21:1-2). The New Jerusalem is the eternal home of the saints and it is described in great detail. It is a beautiful and glorious city that contains features that cannot be explained in human words. For eternity (unmeasurable time) we will worship the King of kings and explore the limitless existence of His creation.

The book of Revelation contains the awesome promise of a glorious future for the believer. As you read it, faith will build (Romans 10:17). Your life, your testimony, and your confessions will be enhanced and strengthened. As the Apostle John said, when you read and hear the words contained in this prophecy, you will be blessed. For this reason, the enemy promotes it as a book of fear, and to him it is. But to you, it is life. Read it and be blessed.

So then faith comes by hearing, and hearing by the word of God.

Romans 10:17

Chapter 15

The Second Coming

For as the lightning comes from the east and flashes to the west, so also will the coming of the Son of Man be.

Matthew 24:27

Before the foundation of the world, and even before the fall of man, God looked forward through the corridors of time with a plan to redeem His creation (1 Peter 1:20-21). The big event that has been the focus of all history and prophecy is the return of the Messiah and Savior of mankind to the earth to defeat the enemy and set up His kingdom. This event is the Second Coming of Christ.

As stated earlier, there are two events that are somewhat similar, one being at the beginning of the Great Tribulation and one being at the end. Both events involve the Church. The first event is the Rapture. This is where Jesus appears in the sky to catch away the bodies, both dead and living, of those who have received Him as their Lord and Savior. These bodies will be caught up into the air and transformed into glorified, resurrected bodies like the body that Jesus received at His glorification. These resurrected and raptured saints with glorified bodies, will then go to Heaven with the Lord and experience the Judgment Seat of Christ and the Marriage Supper of the Lamb.

Jesus Returns with the Saints

The second event is the return of Jesus to earth to set up His kingdom. The raptured saints who now have their glorified, resurrected bodies have been living in Heaven. After seven years, the Lord sends His angels to summon the elect from the far reaches of Heaven. Once assembled and upon the command of the Lord, Christ comes back to earth. Accompanied by His vast army of angels and the saints (the Church), He touches down in Jerusalem on the Mount of Olives.

> *They will see the Son of Man coming on the clouds of heaven with power and great glory. He will send His angels with a great sound of a trumpet, and they will gather together His elect from the four winds, from one end of heaven to the other.*
>
> *Matthew 24:30,31*

In the first event, the Rapture, He comes to earth to get the Church to take the Church to Heaven. In the second event, He returns to earth with the Church to set up His Millennial Kingdom. One takes place before the Tribulation and one takes place after the Tribulation. Again, they are like bookends that mark the beginning and the end of this time of great turmoil on the earth in which the Antichrist attempts to overpower the Son of God and take His kingdom.

The Second Coming

Clearing Up the Confusion

My background is a Baptist background. I was born again at the age of seven during summer Vacation Bible School. The pastor preached to us as young children about the subject of hell. He was very excited in his preaching. In fact, he preached as though he had just gotten back! Later that evening, kneeling next to my mother's bed, I received Jesus as my Lord and Savior.

From that early age, I rarely missed a church service. Our church had two or three revivals per year that lasted for at least two or three weeks each. With evangelical services every night, by the time I was a teenager, I had heard countless sermons about the return of Jesus.

I remember specifically how the passage in Matthew 24 was used to describe the Rapture of the Church (although Jesus is actually referring to His Second Coming in this chapter). It seemed like any scripture that talked about end times was thrown into a pile of scriptures and used to describe the end of days. Although many people received Jesus as their Lord and Savior in those services, the teaching on the end of days seemed very confusing to me. While at the time many scriptures seemed to contradict each other, the reality is they did not. The confusion was a result of the lack of understanding that the Rapture and the Second Coming are two distinct, separate events that take place seven years apart.

Jesus Answers His Disciples

In Matthew 24, when Jesus spoke privately with His disciples on the Mount of Olives, they came to Him with one specific question. They wanted to know what would be the sign of His coming and the end of the age. Since they did not have the concept yet of the Rapture, and because they were Jews, their question was more precisely, "When are You returning to set up Your kingdom?"

In the following passages, Jesus describes the events that will take place near the end of the Tribulation that will signal His descent to the Mount of Olives and the setting up of His Millennial Kingdom.

> *But as the days of Noah were, so also will the coming of the Son of Man be. For as in the days before the flood, they were eating and drinking, marrying and giving in marriage, until the day that Noah entered the ark, and did not know until the flood came and took them all away, so also will the coming of the Son of Man be.*
>
> *Matthew 24:37–39*

> *Immediately after the tribulation of those days the sun will be darkened, and the moon will not give its light; the stars will fall from heaven, and the powers of the heavens will be shaken. Then the sign of the Son of Man will appear in heaven, and then all the tribes of the earth will mourn, and they will see*

*the Son of Man coming on the clouds of heaven with power
and great glory.*

Matthew 24:29,30

Watching for the Signs

On the day of Pentecost after the Holy Spirit had come upon
the 120 believers in the upper room, Peter stood up with the other
eleven disciples and addressed the men of Judea and Jerusalem in
his famous sermon recorded in Acts chapter 2. After explaining
that those who were filled with the Holy Spirit were not drunk
with wine, but instead filled with the Holy Spirit, he quoted the
prophet Joel and prophesied what would take place in the last days.

*I will show wonders in heaven above and signs in the earth
beneath: Blood and fire and vapor of smoke. The sun shall
be turned into darkness, and the moon into blood, before the
coming of the great and awesome Day of the Lord.*

Acts 2:19,20

It's interesting that in this prophetic word, God said that He
would show wonders in Heaven and signs in the earth. He went
on to say that the sun will be turned into darkness and the moon
into blood before the coming of the Lord.

Before Jesus was born in Bethlehem, the prophets of old
prophesied events that would take place before the birth of the
Messiah. Although much of the world went on as usual and did
not recognize the signs of the coming of Jesus, there were those

who had studied the Scriptures and who were watching. They knew from the signs given by the Lord that the Messiah was to be born. The wise men and kings traveled great distances to bring gifts to the infant Jesus. How did they know when to go and where to go? They were watching for the signs. Likewise, in these last days, those of us who study the Bible and watch, we will know.

Touchdown on Earth

And in that day His feet will stand on the Mount of Olives, which faces Jerusalem on the east. And the Mount of Olives shall be split in two, from east to west, making a very large valley; half of the mountain shall move toward the north and half of it toward the south.

Zechariah 14:4

The entire earth will see the Son of Man coming on the clouds of Heaven and the angels of Heaven will sound a trumpet and gather together the chosen ones, all of the righteous, from one end of Heaven to the other. This group, led by the Captain of the Hosts, will descend to the Mount of Olives where the King of kings and the Lord of lords will stand.

The Final Assault

As the Great Tribulation nears its end, the kingdom of darkness makes a final assault. The beast, the false prophet, and the kings of the earth gather their armies to come against the holy city and the kingdom of God. As they are exerting all their power for victory, the door of Heaven opens. The King of kings and Lord of lords is seated on a white horse prepared for battle. The Bible describes His eyes like a flame of fire. He's clothed with a robe dipped in blood. He is the Word of God (Revelation 19:11-13).

> *Now I saw heaven opened, and behold, a white horse. And He who sat on him was called Faithful and True, and in righteousness He judges and makes war. His eyes were like a flame of fire, and on His head were many crowns. He had a name written that no one knew except Himself.*
>
> *Revelation 19:11,12*

As He rides to earth for battle, all of the armies of Heaven, clothed in fine linen, follow Him on white horses. Out of His mouth is a sharp sword and He uses it to strike the nations. The sharp sword, of course, is the Word of God. Jesus used the same weapon when Satan tempted Him three times in the wilderness (Luke 4:8,10,12). Here at the end of the Tribulation, Satan is again defeated by the Word of God.

> *He was clothed with a robe dipped in blood, and His name is called The Word of God. And the armies in heaven, clothed in fine linen, white and clean, followed Him on white horses. Now out of His mouth goes a sharp sword, that with it He should strike the nations. And He himself will rule them with a rod of iron.*
>
> *Revelation 19:13-15*

The beast and the kings of the earth and all of their armies are gathered together for battle to make war against the Lord and His army. But for the enemy, things do not go as planned. The beast, along with the false prophet, will be captured. The false prophet, through signs, is responsible for deceiving everyone who receives the mark of the beast. Both of them will be immediately cast into the lake of fire. The kings and their armies will be killed by the sword that proceeds from the mouth of the Lord who sat on the white horse. The devastation will be so great that the vultures of the earth will be filled with their flesh (Revelation 19:19-21).

I saw the beast, the kings of the earth, and their armies, gathered together to make war against Him who sat on the horse and against His army. Then the beast was captured, and with him the false prophet who worked signs in his presence, by which he deceived those who received the mark of the beast and those who worshiped his image. These two were cast alive into the lake of fire burning with brimstone. And the rest were killed with the sword which proceeded from the mouth of Him who sat on the horse. And all the birds were filled with their flesh.

Revelation 19:19-21

Satan Is Held Captive

After the destruction of the beast, the false prophet, and the kings of the earth, an angel will come down from Heaven holding a key to the bottomless pit. He will also have a great chain with him. This angel will take hold of the dragon, who is the devil and Satan, and will bind him with the chain and cast him into the bottomless pit. The pit will be sealed and locked and for one thousand years (millennium), the devil will be confined to this pit. Hallelujah!

> *Then I saw an angel coming down from heaven, having the key to the bottomless pit and a great chain in his hand. He laid hold of the dragon, that serpent of old, who is the Devil and Satan, and bound him for a thousand years.*
>
> *Revelation 20:1,2*

Resurrection of the Faithful Jews

During the Great Tribulation, the believing remnant of Israel will be protected in the Jordanian desert while waiting for the Messiah. When the Messiah returns and delivers them, the faithful of Israel's past will be resurrected to receive the promise they died believing. God promised that one day he would send a Redeemer and He would dwell with them forever. After the one thousand year reign of the Messiah, the unbelievers will also be resurrected, but to everlasting contempt at the Great White Throne Judgment.

> *At that time Michael shall stand up, the great prince who stands watch over the sons of your people; and there shall be a time of trouble, such as never was since there was a nation, even to that time. And at that time your people shall be delivered, every one who is found written in the book. And many of those who sleep in the dust of the earth shall awake, some to everlasting life, some to shame and everlasting contempt.*
>
> *Daniel 12:1,2*

Resurrection of the Martyred Tribulation Saints

Not only will the King of kings be on His throne, but there will also be other thrones. During the Tribulation, there will be those who will be beheaded because of their witness and because of their faith in God. There will also be those who will be killed because they will not worship the beast or his image and they will not receive the mark of the beast on their foreheads or on their hands. These tribulation saints will be resurrected at this time and they will rule and reign on earth for a thousand years. Remember, the tribulation saints do not have glorified, resurrected bodies so as they rule throughout the Millennium, their thrones will be on earth.

And I saw thrones, and they sat on them, and judgment was committed to them. Then I saw the souls of those who had been beheaded for their witness to Jesus and for the word of God, who had not worshiped the beast or his image, and had not received his mark on their foreheads or on their hands. And they lived and reigned with Christ for a thousand years.

Revelation 20:4

Sheep and Goat Judgment

When the Son of Man comes in His glory, and all the holy angels with Him, then He will sit on the throne of His glory. All the nations will be gathered before Him, and He will separate them one from another, as a shepherd divides his sheep

from the goats. And He will set the sheep on His right hand,
but the goats on the left.

Matthew 25:31-33

Jesus specifically says that when He returns, He will sit on the throne of His glory and that all the nations will stand before Him and He will separate the people as a shepherd divides his sheep. When Jesus returns at the Second Coming to set up His throne on earth, there will be the judgment of the nations. Actually, this is a judgment of the Gentile tribulation survivors.

Of course, the Lord will not judge nations in terms of eternal life. He judges individuals. Throughout history there have been righteous people living in evil nations and evil people living in holy nations. All nations (ethnic groups) will stand before Him and these tribulation survivors will be judged by how they treated "His brothers" (Israel) during the Great Tribulation.

Keep in mind, Jesus was talking to disciples who understood the duties of shepherds in their care for their flocks. Jesus used illustrations and parables that the people of His day would understand.

The Son of Man will take His place on His glorious throne.
Then all the nations will be arranged before Him and He will
sort the people out, much as a shepherd sorts out sheep and
goats, putting sheep to His right and goats to His left.

Matthew 25:31-33 (MSG)

In His description of the judgment that will take place when He enters Jerusalem to take His throne, He is clearly telling His disciples that He will gather all the nations before Him and He will allow the sheep (people) to live in His Millennial Kingdom and He will separate the goats into the everlasting fire prepared for the devil and his angels.

> *Then He will also say to those on the left hand, "Depart from Me, you cursed, into the everlasting fire prepared for the devil and his angels."*

> *Matthew 25:41*

The result will be that the Millennial Kingdom on earth will be inhabited by tribulation saints who received Jesus as their Messiah and blessed the Jews instead of persecuting them during the Tribulation (Matt. 25:37-40).

> *And these will go away into everlasting punishment, but the righteous into eternal life.*

> *Matthew 25:46*

Who Are the Tribulation Saints?

The tribulation saints are those who were unbelievers before the Rapture and were not taken in the Rapture, but remain on the earth in human bodies and receive Jesus as the Messiah during the seven-year Great Tribulation. Some of these saints will be martyred for their faith and some will live until the Second Coming of Jesus. At His return, those martyred for their faith will be resurrected with natural human bodies. They, along with those who were not martyred for their faith and endured to the end, will be counted as sheep. All who are counted as sheep will enter into the Millennium to populate the kingdom of God on earth.

This group is not to be confused with the Church who will have glorified, resurrected bodies that live in the Heavenly Jerusalem. Remember, the Church was saved by grace through faith based upon the work of Jesus (Ephesians 2:8) and were caught up in the Rapture, thus ending the Church age. When the Rapture takes place, the Church is sealed. The tribulation saints are judged by their work of believing and enduring to the end (Matthew 24:13).

To Sum It Up

We give You thanks, O Lord God Almighty, the One who is and who was and who is to come, because You have taken Your great power and reigned. The nations were angry, and Your wrath has come, and the time of the dead, that they should be judged, and that You should reward Your servants the prophets and the saints, and those who fear Your name, small and great, and should destroy those who destroy the earth.

Revelation 11:17,18

There are many more scriptures that describe the Second Coming of Jesus and it would take a book much larger than this to list and illustrate them all. However, with these scriptures that we have discussed, this truth cannot be disputed and is very clear. After the Great Tribulation, Jesus will return to earth. He will separate the tribulation saints (sheep) from the goats. The tribulation saints will move into the Millennium to populate the earth and the goats will be cast into eternal damnation.

We may not know the exact day or the hour of Christ's return, but we definitely know the season. The Scriptures clearly tell us that after the Great Tribulation, the Son of Man will appear in His glory and set up His kingdom. Since we know the Great Tribulation consists of two forty-two month sections totaling seven years, the season of His return is evident. Seven years after the Rapture, He will return, have His angels bind Satan, and set up His Millennial reign.

Chapter 16

The Millennium

One of the most ignored portions of future prophecy is the Millennial reign of Christ. Millennium means one thousand. It is derived from the Latin words *mille* (thousand) and *annus* (year). In biblical terms, it refers to the one thousand year reign of Christ after He returns to earth with His angels and saints to set up His kingdom.

It's a Wonderful Life

As the devastation of the Great Tribulation comes to an end, the devil, his kingdom and all unbelievers have been banished from the earth, and the day that all of Heaven and earth have longed for has come. It will make way for the unprecedented peace on earth that comes with the Millennium. The King of Peace will be ruling with unparalleled strength. He will not allow anything evil to happen under His authority. He will rule with a fist of iron (Revelation 19:15). For those who have evil in their hearts, this will be a time of great restrictions, but for those who love God and give His Son honor as He governs, it will be one thousand years of bliss.

Imagine a world free from theft and murder, where the fear of failure and death are gone. Imagine a world where poisons don't exist and where once-wild animals are tame. Image a world where truth is supreme and deception and "spin" are not possible, because everyone will be judged with the Word of God, which is able to discern the thoughts and intents of the heart (Hebrews 4:12). Common sense will be restored. Imagine a world where you can sing praises freely to the King of kings, where you can pray in public without being ridiculed, and where loving God is the fashionable and "politically-correct" way to live. For the believer, for the one who submits to the King of kings, this will be your world.

The only people who are hindered and restricted by the law are those who desire to break the law. But for those who love God, for them it will be pleasurable to keep His commandments.

Thus says the LORD of hosts: "Old men and old women shall again sit in the streets of Jerusalem, each one with his staff in his hand because of great age. The streets of the city shall be full of boys and girls playing in its streets."

Zechariah 8:4,5

The nursing child shall play by the cobra's hole, and the weaned child shall put his hand in the viper's den. They shall not hurt nor destroy in all My holy mountain, for the earth shall be full of the knowledge of the LORD as the waters cover the sea.

Isaiah 11:8,9

The wolf and lamb shall feed together, the lion shall eat straw as the ox does, and poisonous snakes shall strike no more! In

those days nothing and no one shall be hurt or destroyed in all
my holy mountain, says the LORD.

Isaiah 65:25 (TLB)

Individuality

It has been erroneously portrayed through fictional writings
that in the afterlife people all have identical personalities, looks,
desires, and lifestyle. This is completely wrong. The creation of
God has always been diverse. Of the billions of people on earth,
each one has a unique fingerprint, voice print, and personality. If
God wanted robots, He would have created robots. But He didn't.
He created mankind with great diversity.

As born-again believers, we will not be part of a collective
body like bees in a hive, but as God created us individually, our
individuality will be maintained throughout eternity.

I will give to each a white stone, and on the stone will be
engraved a new name that no one else knows except the one
receiving it.

Revelation 2:17 (TLB)

The Last Uprising

However, as we rule with Him in the Millennium, we will
not specifically be reigning over people who want to be ruled and
reigned over. This is evident because at the end of the Millennium
there will be a great multitude who rebel when they have a leader,

to follow. That leader will be Satan, who will be released from the bottomless pit where he had been held captive since the Second Coming of Jesus and the setting up of His kingdom.

Satan will deceive the nations of the earth, Gog and Magog, and will gather them together for battle. The Bible says that their number will be so great that it will be like the sand of the sea (Revelation 21:8). As they go up and surround the camp of the earthly saints in Jerusalem, God sends down fire from Heaven and they are devoured.

Now when the thousand years have expired, Satan will be released from his prison and will go out to deceive the nations which are in the four corners of the earth, Gog and Magog, to gather them together to battle, whose number is as the sand of the sea. They went up on the breadth of the earth and surrounded the camp of the saints and the beloved city. And fire came down from God out of heaven and devoured them.

Revelation 20:7-9

I think it is interesting that the enemy who was originally in the Paradise of God in Heaven before man was created, the enemy who tempted Jesus in the wilderness, the enemy who is responsible for all disease, poverty, and every kind of evil experienced by mankind, the enemy who created havoc on the earth during the Great Tribulation, and the enemy who gathered an army as great as the sand of the sea is destroyed by God in one half of a verse (Revelation 20:9).

The enemy doesn't realize as he is gathering his army for battle that he is actually gathering them together for their destruction.

I'm quite sure that people could look at this great army and see it as undefeatable. But as believers, we must never look at the size of the enemy or at the circumstances, but instead put our trust in the promise of God. He gave those who believe authority over all the power of the enemy and He said that nothing would hurt them (Luke 10:19).

As a person trusting in God, we must believe and stand in faith that His Word is true. Light always overpowers darkness and we are children of the light.

Who Makes up the Great Army of Satan?

Children who are born during the Millennium will not be saved on the coattails of their parents' beliefs, but they must make their own decision. The responsibility of individual choice did not end with the Church age but continues throughout the Millennium. Their judgment and acceptance to continue to live on earth past the end of the Millennial Kingdom into the eternal kingdom will be determined by their personal belief in the Messiah. They will not get a free pass because of the belief of their parents.

The earth will be populated during the millennium by those who were judged as sheep and allowed to enter in. They will still be in natural bodies, susceptible to desires of the flesh, and their children will be born in natural human bodies. Choices will be made and some will choose evil.

Although the earth will be under the rulership of King Jesus and the glorified Church, there will still be a subculture of rebellion that will be easily deceived when Satan is released at the end of the one thousand year reign. It may be difficult to believe that anyone would sin on an earth ruled by the King of Peace, but keep in mind that those living in their natural bodies on the earth have not yet been judged at the final judgment of man.

Everything on the earth during the Millennium will not be like it is in Heaven. While Heaven will remain pure and undefiled because it is inhabited by resurrected saints and angels of God, the earth is still inhabited by fleshly man.

Remember, the first generation in the Millennium will have experienced the evil and the persecution of the Antichrist. This first generation will be very thankful to be alive and living under the rule of the King of kings. However, as history has shown us, within one generation, attitudes and agendas change.

The generation that fought the Nazis during World War II is what I call the hero generation. Stories have been written and they have even been called the greatest generation. Young men from the east coast to the west coast, from north to south left the cities and their farms for a common cause. The nation was united and there was a single purpose. Patriotism was at an all-time high. When the war ended in victory, the surviving soldiers were greeted with parades at home and those who had fallen in service were honored in memorials across the nation for their ultimate sacrifice.

Twenty years later, American young men and women fought and died, but also many fled to Canada to avoid military service. The term "draft dodger" was a common term. As soldiers who had fought and risked their lives for the nations in the swamps of Vietnam returned home, many were pelted with garbage as they stepped onto American soil. The American flag that had been honored for generations was being burned in the streets publicly by this new generation.

In one generation of twenty years, the victories and heroes of the greatest generation were forgotten and were replaced with attitudes of contempt. If this can happen in twenty years in a free nation, then it certainly can happen within a thousand years, especially when the great deceiver is released from his prison.

Of course, not everyone will be deceived. There will be a great multitude on earth who honor the kingdom of God and give praise to the King of kings. There will be those who will continue to believe God and His Word. The Word of God, the Holy Bible, that we have now will not be extinct. It will, of course, still be in use on the earth during the Millennium and there will be those who read the Word and believe the Word just like there are those today who read the Word and believe the Word. But also just like today, there will be those who do not, and they will be susceptible to the lies of the devil when he is released.

Deception is one of the greatest tools of Satan. He will gather his army from those who have distanced themselves from the things of God and in doing so will fall prey to his lies. Like one-third of the angels in Heaven, he will convince them that he can somehow overthrow God.

The Miracle of Israel

When I was born in 1947, the nation of Israel did not exist. When I was born, there were 48 states. My grandchildren think that when I was born, Moses was in diapers! But the reality is, it was not that long ago. In these last few decades, major prophetic developments have taken place on the earth.

My great-grandfather was a circuit rider. He traveled through the Ozarks of Missouri with his Bible and study books in his saddlebag. He was a great man who was a teacher and a preacher.

Many years ago, I was given two of the books he carried in his saddlebag that he used for a basis of his Bible study. They were published near the turn of the century before World War I. From time to time I enjoy looking at his books called *The Biblical Educator*. They are hard bound, well worn, and heavily marked from his studies.

While glancing through one of his study guides, I saw the statement about the prophesies concerning the nation of Israel. This study guide said that even though the Bible says that the people of Israel will be drawn back into the Promised Land and become a nation again, in reality this would not physically happen. The writer went on to say that what the Bible really means is that all of the Jewish people in the world would be drawn to Israel in their hearts and that the Bible was speaking metaphorically and not literally.

There is a dangerous area that many Bible scholars could fall into. While it is true that the Bible contains types and shadows and parables, we cannot take the prophecies of the Word and ignore them or explain them away because of the perceived impossibility that they will happen. When God's Word prophesies future events, they are not to be taken as metaphorical fairy tales, but to be looked upon as actual events that will take place in God's prophetic timetable.

What the writers of my great-grandfather's study guide couldn't believe came to pass within five decades of their writing. On May 14, 1948, with great personal, political, and strategic concerns, President Harry Truman from Missouri announced to the world American recognition of the new state of Israel. On May 15, 1948, it became official that Israel had joined the family of nations on the earth. Immediately that day, Israel was attacked. This small nation that is no larger than the state of New Jersey soundly defeated the armies of Lebanon, Egypt, Syria, Transjordan, and Iraq.

In 1967, Israel defeated the armies from the neighboring states of Egypt (known at the time as the United Arab Republic), Jordan, and Syria within six days and recaptured Jerusalem. In 1973, Israel was attacked on Yom Kippur by the coalition of Arab states led by Egypt and Syria. The enemy thought by attacking Israel on their holy day that they would be caught off guard and easily defeated. But the enemies of Israel were once again surprised and soundly defeated.

To this day, the enemies of Israel continue to attack God's chosen people. The enemy has a purpose in this. He believes if he can eliminate the Jews, he can keep the prophecies of the Bible from coming to pass because the Jews are included and very prominent in end time prophetic events from now through eternity.

For almost 2,000 years prior to 1948, the nation of Israel had not had a national currency, language, or army and to top it off, the land that the Bible said they would inherit was occupied by enemies who hated them and desired to kill them. So to think that Israel could actually become a nation again under these circumstances was impossible for most Bible scholars to believe. But regardless of the belief of man who alters the Word based on conditions or political correctness, when God says something will happen, it will happen.

With the miracle of Israel now behind us, we can clearly see that the God of Abraham, Isaac, and Jacob, that the God who raised Jesus from the dead, that the God who cleansed us from our sin by the blood of His Son will do what He said He would do. What He has prophesied in His Word to mankind will be literally accomplished.

God did not symbolically create man and Jesus did not symbolically go to prepare a place for us. We will not symbolically be raptured, and the devil will not symbolically be defeated. All of these events are literal and God's prophetic future will play out as He has spoken it will.

The Purpose of the Millennium

Some people question why there even is a Millennium, and why Satan is released at the end of the thousand years. They wonder why God doesn't just eliminate evil at the Second Coming and move into eternity. Here is what I believe to be the purpose of the Millennium.

1) To fulfill the prophecy of God's timetable for man

As discussed near the beginning of this book, God created the heavens and the earth in six days and on the seventh day He rested. In His written Word, the Holy Scriptures, we are clearly told that with God one day is as a thousand years and a thousand years as a day. God said that man's days on the earth would be 120 years. Again as discussed in chapter 2, 120 Jubilee years equal 6,000 years on man's timetable. From the time Adam was kicked out of the garden until the return of the Messiah to set up His kingdom is 6,000 years, followed by the Day of the Lord, the Millennial reign. In order for prophecy to be fulfilled, this must take place.

2) To put an end, once and for all, to evil and death

Although Satan is bound for the one thousand years, at the end of the Millennium he, all evil, and death are cast into the lake of fire. From that point on throughout eternity, there will be no more Satan and there will be no more death.

3) To insure all humanity has a choice

Before the Second Coming, all humanity has had life and death placed before them and they had to choose, either by grace or by works depending upon the dispensation they were in. Those living in the Millennial Kingdom will likewise need to make a choice to be for God or against Him before the eternal kingdom begins after the revelation of the new Heaven and earth. For this to be possible, evil is allowed on the earth again for a short time to allow the millennial generation to make the choice.

4) To show the goodness of God to mankind

The glory that God has given to His Church, the magnificence of their glorified, resurrected bodies, and the goodness of God to humanity still living on the earth during the Millennium will be a stark contrast to the evil that has ravaged the earth through the six days of man.

On this seventh day, the Millennial Day of the Lord, the light of the Almighty will shine so brightly that His goodness will be evident to all. However, during the Day of the Lord, as glorious as it is, mankind will still have a choice of whether to worship the Creator of light or the creature of darkness. As always, God says, "Before you I have placed life and death. Please choose Me. I am the life and the light."

Chapter 17

The Great White Throne Judgment

And I saw a great white throne, and him that sat on it, from whose face the earth and the heaven fled away; and there was found no place for them. And I saw the dead, small and great, stand before God; and the books were opened: and another book was opened, which is the book of life: and the dead were judged out of those things which were written in the books, according to their works.

And the sea gave up the dead which were in it; and death and hell delivered up the dead which were in them: and they were judged every man according to their works. And death and hell were cast into the lake of fire. This is the second death. And whosoever was not found written in the book of life was cast into the lake of fire.

Revelation 20:11–15

Throughout the Bible, there are many judgments and there are several that are still to take place in the future. However, I would like to only focus here on two of the future judgments of mankind. Although at these two judgments, each person will be judged individually, they are completely different in time and purpose. These two judgments are the Judgment Seat of Christ and the Great White Throne Judgment.

Throughout my life as a minister, I have heard many sermons that were confusing, unscriptural, and promoted fear. For the Church, these judgments should not bring fear, but instead, bring great rejoicing. Although the Judgment Seat of Christ was described in detail in Chapter 13, for comparison's sake, let's take a moment and examine these two judgments.

The Two Judgments of Man

Simply put, there are two major judgments of man in Heaven.

• The Judgment Seat of Christ

This first judgment takes place shortly after the Rapture. Everyone at this judgment has already received eternal life and they will receive rewards based upon their deeds on earth.

• The Great White Throne Judgment

This last judgment takes place at the end of the Millennium. Everyone at this judgment will be judged by their works and not by the grace of God. Those who are judged worthy will enter into the eternal kingdom and those whose names are not found written in the Book of Life who are judged unworthy will be cast into the lake of fire (Revelation 20:15).

You can see the difference in these two judgments. One is a rewards judgment at the Rapture for the Church and the other is a works judgment at the end of the Millennium. As a human being, you will be at only one of these judgments.

The Judgment for the Righteous

The Judgment Seat of Christ takes place shortly after the Rapture and obviously is only for those who are born again and caught up in the Rapture. This judgment is not to judge your salvation. Your eternal life has already been predetermined if you are at this judgment. As a Christian, your eternal life began the moment you received Jesus as your Lord and Savior.

Remember, your salvation is based upon the obedience and sacrifice of Jesus. Your salvation is not judged at the Judgment Seat of Christ. However, at the Great White Throne Judgment, those attending will have their salvation judged and it will be based upon their works and not the grace of God.

The Great White Throne Judgment

At the end of the Millennium, Satan will be released for a short while and he will deceive many on the earth. There will be those who will accept his deception and fight in his army against God and His holy city. Likewise, there will be those living on the earth who will reject his deception and continue to honor and worship God. After fire comes down and destroys the army of Satan, there will be a resurrection of all of the unrighteous dead and they, along with those living on the earth, will be judged. This final judgment of mankind is called the Great White Throne Judgment.

At this judgment, the unrighteous dead who have been held in the heart of the earth in a place called Hades and those who are deceived by Satan and become a part of His army will be judged and cast into the lake of fire. The righteous living on the earth will move into the eternal kingdom to populate the new earth. More clearly, this judgment will be a final declaration on all of those who have rejected Jesus as the Son of God, the Messiah, and as Lord.

As the seventh day of man's days on the earth closes and preparation is being made for mankind to step into eternity with God, the resurrection of the unrighteous dead and the Great White Throne Judgment must be completed.

> *But the rest of the dead did not live again until the thousand years were finished.*

> *Revelation 20:5*

> *But the heaven we see now and the earth we live on now have been kept by His word. They will be kept until they are to be destroyed by fire. They will be kept until the day men stand before God and sinners will be destroyed.*

> *2 Peter 3:7 (NLV)*

The Afterlife of the Unrighteous

As a minister with decades of ministry, I have had many people ask me about what happens to those who do not accept Jesus as their

Lord and die without Christ. Let's take a moment and examine the afterlife of the unrighteous.

When Jesus told of the rich man and Lazarus, we know that Lazarus was in Paradise and is now in Heaven. But what about the rich man? We know that the thief on the cross who acknowledged Jesus as the Messiah went to Paradise with Jesus that very day and is now in Heaven. But what about the other thief who rejected Jesus? Both of these unrighteous men were born and died under the Old Covenant. Angels did not escort them to Paradise. They simply went to Hades in the heart of the earth and that's where they are now.

Likewise, under the New Covenant, the unrighteous go to Hades. All of mankind enters into Hades as a result of unrighteousness and remains there through the Rapture, through the Great Tribulation, through the Second Coming, and through the Millennial reign of Christ. These unrighteous spirits in torment in Hades will be resurrected and stand before God individually and will be judged unworthy.

Regardless of a man's works on earth, only one – the second Adam, Jesus – was righteous enough to place His blood on the altar in Heaven. Those who received His sacrifice and believed in Him were made righteous because of His act of obedience.

Everyone who will be at the White Throne Judgment will be from one of three groups:

1) Unrighteous before the sacrifices of Jesus because they had no faith in God.

2) Unrighteous under the New Covenant because they rejected the cleansing blood of Jesus.

3) Lived on earth during the Millennium and have not been through a previous judgment.

The eternal damnation of the devil has already been proclaimed by God. Likewise the destiny of the fallen angels who were the unclean demonic spirits on earth has already been decided. It is as though their eternal death has been determined and they have been on death row for thousands of years waiting for the final execution that separates them from God and seals their torment for all eternity. Although hell was not created for man, but instead was created for Satan and his angels, those who are judged unrighteous at the Great White Throne Judgment will have the same eternal separation from God and righteous mankind.

At this point, evil is forever banished, the righteous have been vindicated, death is destroyed, and from then on, the King of Kings rules forever and ever and ever.

Chapter 18

The New Jerusalem and Eternity

Now I saw a new heaven and a new earth, for the first heaven and the first earth had passed away. Also there was no more sea. Then I, John, saw the holy city, New Jerusalem, coming down out of heaven from God, prepared as a bride adorned for her husband.

Revelation 21:1,2

Renovated, Not Different

I n Koine Greek (New Testament Greek), there are two words translated "*new*" in our English Bible. They are *neos* and *kainos*. *Neos* means new in time, something that has never been in existence before. *Kainos* means new in nature or something that has been refurbished and improved.

An example of this is in 2 Corinthians 5:17 where it says that if anyone is in Christ that old things have passed away and everything has become new. The Greek word for new used in this passage is *kainos*. When Paul uses *kainos* in the expression new creation, he did not intend to imply that this is a completely different individual.

He meant that there was continuity between the old person and the new person to such an extent that it remains the same person, but renovated. The person is the same, but the quality of that person has been transformed.

With this in mind, in Revelation 21:1, the Greek word used for a new heaven, a new earth, and New Jerusalem is *kainos*. The new heaven, the new earth, and the New Jerusalem are not a different heaven, a different earth, and a different Heavenly Jerusalem, but they are all restored, refurbished, and upgraded to brand new condition.

The New Jerusalem

In Revelation 20, John was approached by one of the seven angels who had the seven bowls with the seven plagues. The angel said to him, *"Come and I will show you the bride, the Lamb's wife"* (Revelation 21:9). Then John was taken away by the Holy Spirit to a very high mountain and while standing there, he saw the holy Jerusalem descending out of Heaven, covered with the glory of God.

The city glowed. John described it as a light that was like a precious jasper stone, but clear as crystal. Then he saw that surrounding the city was a very great and high wall with twelve gates. There was an angel at each gate and each gate had a name written on it. The twelve names on the twelve gates were the twelve names of the twelve tribes of the children of Israel. Three gates were on the east, three gates were on the north, three gates on the south, and three gates on the west (Revelation 21:11-13).

Keep in mind we are talking about a city in Heaven, not the entirety of Heaven. The wall of the city had twelve foundations and on these twelve foundations were the names of the twelve apostles of the Lamb. As John was walking and talking with his guide, he was handed a gold reed and he was told to measure the city, the gates, and its wall. When he did, here's what he discovered. The city itself was laid out in a perfect square. The height, the width, and the length were all the same measurement (Revelation 21:14-16).

The Bible says that the length, width, and height were each 12,000 furlongs. In the original manuscripts, the word translated as furlong was actually the Greek word *stadia* and 12,000 stadia is about 1,380 miles. John went on to describe the beauty of the city and he likened the walls, the gates, and the street of the city as very precious stones, pearls, and gold (Revelation 21:16-21).

Replacement Theology

Throughout my life I have encountered people who were anti-Semitic. For some reason they had allowed the spirit of the enemy to turn their hearts against the chosen people of God. Although every church has a Bible that includes Genesis 12:3 that says, "*I will bless those who bless you, and I will curse him who curses you; and in you all the families of the earth shall be blessed,*" yet some still allow themselves to speak evil of the nation of Israel.

There is a theological term called Replacement Theology. This is the belief that the Christian church has replaced the Jews and that the Jews are no longer heirs to the promises of God. They believe that somehow God has forsaken His covenant with them and given it to the Church.

It's very evident that as the New Jerusalem descends out of Heaven from God, that God has named the twelve gates with the names of the twelve tribes of Israel. Every born-again believer who is a part of the Church will for all eternity enter and exit through those gates. This alone is a good reminder that God is not finished with the nation of Israel and that Israel has a place in the eternal future. So, I would suggest if you have any anti-Semitism of any type in you, ask for forgiveness and repent because Heaven is a very Jewish place.

Eternity

Usually when we think about eternity, we think of a future that never ends. However, there is also eternity past. In the same way that the future is limitless without end, so is the past – limitless and without beginning. While we may intellectually know this, we cannot fully grasp the reality of it.

When did eternity start? It didn't. Eternity has always been and eternity will always be. God lives in eternity and time was carved out of eternity and created for man. There will be a time when time as we know it will cease to exist; however, it will be at least one thousand years from now before eternity begins.

All science requires a foundational marker, a point of contact, that anchors the truth so that all other truths can be measured. But eternity has no anchor or foundation. It just is. Is what? Eternity is forever past and forever future, anchored only in God.

The Circle of Time

In the western way of thinking, time is linear. However, the ancient Hebrew concept of time is that time is circular and eventually circles back upon itself, making it never ending. In the same way that a traditional clock is not a time line, but the hands move in a circular motion and eventually return to the same position, the ancient Hebrews of the Bible did not see time with a singular defined beginning and end. They saw time as a continual cycle of beginnings and endings, like a helix.

A helix is a scientific term describing a three dimensional spiral curve. In the same way that threads on a bolt continually circle the bolt, without touching or overlapping but move upward, the Hebrew concept of time is also circular in nature, with a continual unending movement upward toward God.

Because the western culture sees time as linear, it's much more difficult to understand the continual unending concept of time. With a circular view of time, our perspective of the beginning and end of earth and man's days on the earth changes.

Earthly Time vs. Eternity

Eternity doesn't mean that the measurement of time will not exist, but the urgency that time brings on earth will not exist. Time in eternity, unlike time on earth, will not be accompanied by aging, deterioration, decay, or deadlines.

So at the end of a month on earth in the timeline of man, a man will be one month older with his body aging. One month will be marked off of his future and placed into his past because the number of months on the earth are limited. A man living on the earth in his physical human body progresses through the timeline of his appointed years that span between physical birth and physical death. With the passing of each year there is one additional year in his past and one less year in his future.

In eternity, after passing a marker of time, there will be no less days in the future than there were before passing the marker because the future days are limitless. Thus time has no effect.

Of course, there must be a measurement of time in the kingdom of God. Otherwise, the eternal feasts and holy days that God said would be celebrated forever on certain days could not be done (Exodus 12:14).

Although time must be sequenced and have markers, it will be eternal without beginning or end. Like the immortal song "Amazing Grace" says, "When we've been there 10,000 years, bright shining as the sun, we've no less days to sing God's praise than when we first begun."

Conclusion

If you are a born-again believer in Jesus Christ, if you have accepted Him as your Lord and Savior, then as a Christian, your future is bright. Atheists and unbelievers will have no hope, but you will have total assurance of your destiny.

At the moment your body ceases to function, you will be escorted into the presence of the Lord in Heaven where you will experience fullness of joy waiting for the day that Jesus appears in the sky, whereupon your dead body will be resurrected and brought back to glorious life. When that event takes place and you re-enter Heaven, you will obtain your individual rewards and then feast at the Marriage Supper of the Lamb.

While you are celebrating in Heaven, great tribulation takes place on the earth. When it looks like the enemy is about to set up his kingdom in Jerusalem, you will return to earth with Jesus, the enemy will be defeated and bound and you will rule and reign with Jesus in your glorified, resurrected body out of the Heavenly Jerusalem for the next one thousand years. And just when you think things couldn't get any better, they do.

Although the enemy is released for a short time, he is defeated and eternally judged. Heaven and earth is renewed and the New Jerusalem descends out of Heaven from God, containing the place that Jesus prepared for you in His Father's house. For all eternity you, in your glorified, resurrected body, will be with the Lord Jesus and experience the things that Paul said were so magnificent that earthly words could not describe them. As a believer in the Lord Jesus Christ, your best days are yet to come.

It's Your Choice

The angels in Heaven made a choice and one-third of them chose poorly and received eternal destruction. Adam and Eve made a choice and they chose poorly and were cast out of the Garden of God. Now it is your time to choose. Will your choice be wise or will you choose poorly?

There's a choice and there's a separation. Goats on the left (destruction), sheep on the right (enter into the eternal kingdom). God said that He has placed before us life and death and then He says, *"Choose life."*

The Final Victory

The greatest fear of mankind has always been death. Every fear experienced throughout history is a result of the looming presence of death.

But in the end, the last enemy to be destroyed by the King of kings and the Lord of lords is death itself. As Paul said, until we get there, earthly words cannot describe the magnitude of the Kingdom of Heaven where we will forever be in the presence of our Lord and forever separated from the power and sting of death.

For as in Adam all die, even so in Christ all shall be made alive. But each one in his own order: Christ the firstfruits, afterward those who are Christ's at His coming.

Then comes the end, when He delivers the kingdom to God the Father, when He puts an end to all rule and all authority and power.

For He must reign till He has put all enemies under His feet. The last enemy that will be destroyed is death.

1 Corinthians 15:22–26

The Hallelujah Chorus
George Frideric Handel

Hallelujah! For the Lord God omnipotent reigneth.

(Revelation 19:6)

The kingdom of this world is become the Kingdom of our Lord, and of His Christ; and He shall reign for ever and ever.

(Revelation 11:15)

KING OF KINGS, LORD OF LORDS.

(Revelation 19:16)

How Do I Become Born Again?

Behold, now is the accepted time; behold, now is the day of salvation.

(2 Corinthians 6:2)

There is only one way to have everlasting life, to live forever and be assured you will always be with the Lord. There is only one way to the kingdom of God, the kingdom of Heaven, and to the Father. That one way is – Jesus.

God loved you so much that He sent Jesus to earth to pay the price for your sins and make a way for you to live forever with Him. He paid the price you could not pay. He made a way of escape from the bondage of sin and death, and from the coming wrath. Receiving the gift of salvation and becoming a part of the Church is simple. Read these four basic steps and the scriptures, then pray and accept the gift of salvation.

1) **You Must Believe in Jesus**. You must believe that Jesus is the Son of God and that God raised Him from the dead. This is the basis of our Christian faith.

For God so loved the world that He gave His only begotten Son, that whoever believes in Him should not perish but have everlasting life. For God did not send His Son into the world to condemn the world, but that the world through Him might be saved John 3:16,17.

Believe on the Lord Jesus Christ, and you will be saved, you and your household Acts 16:31.

2) You Must Confess Your Sins. You must acknowledge that you are a sinner and you want Jesus to wash your sins away.

If we confess our sins, He is faithful and just to forgive us our sins and to cleanse us from all unrighteousness (1 John 1:9).

3) You Must Repent. Repent means to turn away from your sins and stop doing them. Romans 6:23 says, *"For the wages of sin is death but the gift of God is eternal life in Christ Jesus our Lord."* The payment for sin is death, but when you accept Jesus and repent of your sins, you receive eternal life.

The time is fulfilled, and the kingdom of God is at hand. Repent, and believe in the gospel (Mark 1:15).

4) You Must Confess Jesus Before Men. You must publicly acknowledge you have accepted Jesus and never deny Him.

If you confess with your mouth the Lord Jesus and believe in your heart that God has raised Him from the dead, you will be saved. For with the heart one believes unto righteousness, and with the mouth confession is made unto salvation (Romans 10:9,10).

Therefore whoever confesses Me before men, him I will also confess before My Father who is in heaven. But whoever denies Me before men, him I will also deny before My Father who is in heaven (Matthew 10:32,33).

For by grace you have been saved through faith, and that not of yourselves; it is the gift of God (Ephesians 2:8).

But as many as received Him, to them He gave the right to

become children of God, even to those who believe in His name (John 1:12).

Jesus said, "I say to you that likewise there will be more joy in heaven over one sinner who repents than over ninety-nine just persons who need no repentance" (Luke 15:7).

PRARYER OF SALVATION

God loves you—no matter who you are, no matter what
your past. God loves you so much that He gave His one and only
begotten Son for you. The Bible tells us that "...whoever
believes in Him shall not perish but have eternal life" (John 3:16
NIV). Jesus laid down His life and rose again so that we could
spend eternity with Him in heaven and experience His absolute
best on earth. If you would like to receive Jesus into your life,
say the following prayer out loud and mean it from your heart.

*Heavenly Father, I come to You admitting that I am
a sinner. Right now, I choose to turn away from sin, and
I ask You to cleanse me of all unrighteousness. I believe
that Your Son, Jesus, died on the cross to take away my
sins. I also believe that He rose again from the dead so
that I might be forgiven of my sins and made righteous
through faith in Him. I call upon the name of Jesus
Christ to be the Savior and Lord of my life. Jesus, I
choose to follow You and ask that You fill me with the
power of the Holy Spirit. I declare that right now I am
a child of God. I am free from sin and full of the righteousness of God. I am saved in Jesus' name. Amen.*

If you prayed this prayer to receive Jesus Christ as your
Savior for the first time, please contact us on the Web at
www.harrisonhouse.com to receive a free book.

Or you may write to us at
Harrison House • P.O. Box 35035 • Tulsa, Oklahoma 74153

Bibliography

Ariel, Israel and Chaim Richman. *Carta's Illustrated Encyclopedia of the Holy Temple in Jerusalem.* Jerusalem, Israel: Carta, Jerusalem, 2005.

Sherman, Rabbi Nosson. *The Chumash.* Brooklyn, NY: Menorah Publications, LTD., 2000.

About the Author

Dr. Larry Ollison is founder and Senior Pastor of Walk on the Water Faith Church and founder of Larry Ollison Ministries. With over forty years in the ministry, Dr. Ollison ministers the Word of Faith through radio, television, internet and daily e-mail devotionals. The author of seven books including The Power of Grace, The Practical Handbook for Christian Living and Life is in the Blood, he is a very popular speaker nationally and internationally.

www.larryollison.org

Appendix